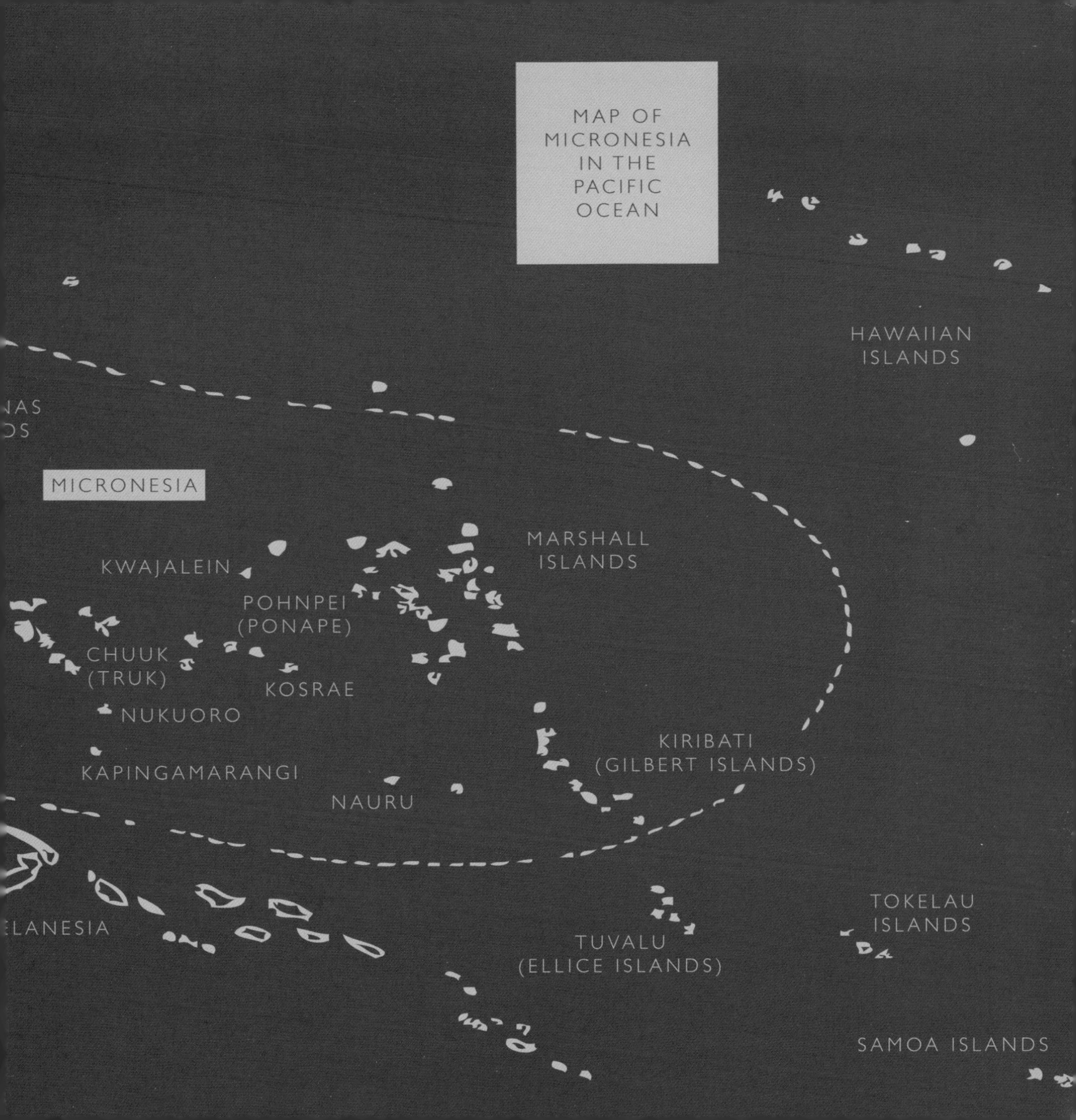

MAP OF
MICRONESIA
IN THE
PACIFIC
OCEAN

HAWAIIAN
ISLANDS

MICRONESIA

NAS
OS

MARSHALL
ISLANDS

KWAJALEIN

POHNPEI
(PONAPE)

CHUUK
(TRUK)

KOSRAE

NUKUORO

KAPINGAMARANGI

NAURU

KIRIBATI
(GILBERT ISLANDS)

ELANESIA

TUVALU
(ELLICE ISLANDS)

TOKELAU
ISLANDS

SAMOA ISLANDS

ARTS AND CRAFTS OF MICRONESIA

TRADING WITH TRADITION

3565 HARDING AVENUE
HONOLULU, HAWAI'I 96816
808.734.7159 • WWW.BESSPRESS.COM

BARBARA
WAVELL

Copyright © 2010 by Bess Press, Inc.
3565 Harding Avenue
Honolulu, Hawai'i 96816

COVER AND BOOK DESIGN: CATHERINE AU HOY

Cataloging-in-publication data
Wavell, Barbara.
 Arts and crafts of Micronesia : trading
with tradition / by Barbara Wavell.
    p.   cm.
 Includes illustrations.
 ISBN-13: 978-157306-3098
 ISBN-10: 157306-3096
 1. Arts—Micronesia. 2. Arts—Oceania.
3. Handicraft—Micronesia. 4. Ethnology—
Micronesia. 5. Micronesia—Social life and
customs. I. Title.
NX596.M5.W38 2010   700.965-dc22

Printed and bound in China through Colorcraft Ltd., Hong Kong

Acknowledgement of Support: This project has been financed in part with Historic Preservation Funds in partnership with the US National Park Service, US Department of the Interior, and Federated States of Micronesia Historic Preservation Program.

Disclaimer: The contents and opinions expressed do not necessarily reflect the views or policies of the US Department of the Interior, and Federated States of Micronesia Historic Preservation Program.

Non Discrimination and Equal Opportunity: This program received Federal funds from the US National Park Service. Regulations of the US Federally Assisted Programs strictly prohibit unlawful discrimination on the basis of race, color, national origin, age, sex, sexual orientation, or handicap. Any person who believes that he or she has been discriminated against in any program, activity or facility operated by a recipient of Federal assistance should write to: Director, Equal Opportunity Program, US Department of Interior National Park Service, PO Box 37127, Washington DC 20013-7127.

FIGURE 1

FIGURE 2

FIGURE 3

Over thirty years ago, while shopping in a flea market, I found my first storyboard and, later, my first "monkeyman." However, when I wanted to learn more about these mysterious and, to me, very attractive cultural objects, information was difficult to find. The storyboard was said to be from Kwajalein in the Marshall Islands. I later learned that such storyboards originated in Palau, but, after WWII and during the Trust Territory period, handicrafts were imported throughout the islands. Thus, the storyboard had been brought to the large U.S. military base at Kwajalein to be sold at the "Mic Shop." This was one of the early challenges in the identification of Micronesian handicrafts. One could never assume that they had originated in the location from which they were purchased. But, with a Master of Arts degree in cultural anthropology earned in 1979, before the computer age of research, I knew the kinds of places to look for information. I ordered many books and articles through interlibrary loan or bought them second hand, until, over a period of years, I had accumulated my own specialized library. The computer age enabled both research and acquisition, and, as I encountered more and more interesting items from the diverse region known as Micronesia, I was able to compare different ages and styles of objects such as baskets, fans, and statues to see how styles and techniques had changed through time and across locations. The main sources of these items have included military personnel, island administrators, missionaries, and tourists who have brought back memories of their travels in the form of island arts, crafts, and tools. Most commonly, the time period for the objects has been from the 1940s to the present, although I have obtained older items when possible. My collection has been exhibited at the Maitland Art Center in 1996, the Museum of Arts and Sciences in Daytona Beach, Florida in 2002, and the University of Central Florida Library in 2004. The research involved in creating my collection has taken me on an extremely rewarding journey, thanks to the wonderful, dedicated, interesting, and helpful people I have had the pleasure of getting to know along the way.

First, thanks to my husband, Kane Lamberty, and daughter, Lindsey, for being patient, both with my collection and my studies. Thanks to my mother, Joan Wavell, and mother-in-law, Jackie Lamberty, for their continual support and interest. A special thanks to my late father-in-law, Harry Lamberty, who spent hours and hours restoring many of the outrigger canoe models in the collection. Thanks to all the people who have helped me directly with my research: the late Kempis Mad, formerly a research assistant at the Belau National Museum; Father Fran Hezel and the Micronesian Seminar, for making photos available and providing a supportive sounding board for my research and publication efforts; Mary McCutcheon, who provided information about holdings at the Smithsonian Institution; Hera Ware Owen, who has been a continual source of support and information in many ways; Mandy Etpison, who made me welcome in 2004 during the Ninth Festival of Pacific Arts; Faustina Rehuher from the Belau National Museum, for her helpful advice on copyright; Lonnie Fread, at the Yap Art Studio and Gallery, whose website and quick response have provided a solid source for information about Yap; Dr. Donald Rubinstein, who shares my interests; Dr. Peter Black, for his help with Tobi topics; Dr. Eric Metzgar, an early sounding board on Chuuk and figural sculpture; Ron Mayo, for early proofreading help and generosity; Dr. Mac Marshall and Dr. James Nason, who have assisted with research on the material culture of Chuuk; Kathleen Montvel-Cohen, for sharing information about carvers; Jerry Shepp, former director of the Maitland Art Center, who sponsored my first exhibit and obtained funding for a catalog to go with it; Jonathan Fogel, editor of Tribal Arts Magazine, for his support of my research and publication efforts; Dr. Martha

C. Ward, for sharing her experiences and photos of souvenirs from Pohnpei; Jeannie Latenser, a former Peace Corps worker who gathered information for me about fans on Kosrae; Diane Goodwillie, for providing information on Kiribati handicraft resources; Bill Perryclear, for providing information and samples of Palauan baskets; numerous anthropologists on ASAONET, who have been generous with their time and experience; and all others who so generously shared their collections and their knowledge with me. Some of you may be mentioned in endnotes in association with specific objects. Thanks to Seventh-day Adventist missionaries Rus and Marilyn Aldridge for their support, including sharing their accommodations with me during the Ninth Festival of Pacific Arts. Thanks to Buddy Bess of Bess Press, for taking an interest in this project; to copyeditor Karyl Reynolds, for being a pleasure to work with; to Paula Creech (U.S. Department of the Interior), for her unfailing support and council in shepherding me through the grant process; to Resty Shotaro, Historic Preservation Officer of the Federated States of Micronesia; to the staff of the Historic Preservation Office of the Federated States of Micronesia (especially Jenny); and to the government of the Federated States of Micronesia, who generously supported this project. A special thank you to photographer Tim Dunlap, who took many of the photographs of objects found in this work, and to artist K. C. Weller, who drew the excellent map. Finally, to all the artists and artisans of Micronesia who have created things of beauty, quality, and cultural meaning, please accept my enduring respect and appreciation.

Micronesia encompasses a vast area of the Pacific Ocean and includes many island cultures well adapted to their specialized environments. The twentieth century was a turbulent period in Micronesian history with intervals of colonial rule under Spain, Germany, and Japan, and, finally, administration by the United States as the Trust Territory of the Pacific Islands. By the end of the century, many Micronesian nations attained their independence and opted for free association with the U.S., spelled out in the Compact of Free Association. Through many changes in administration, handicraft production has continued to be important to the cultures of Micronesia. This book celebrates the creativity of Micronesian artists into the twenty-first century. Arts and artifacts illustrated here come from the Barbara B. Wavell Collection. Most of these intriguing items were originally acquired by U.S. military personnel and administrators who visited Micronesia during and in the decades immediately after WWII, when Micronesia was known as the Trust Territory. This work sets out to evaluate different categories of art, including figural sculpture, storyboards, baskets, bowls, fans, clothing, jewelry, model outrigger canoes, and other Oceanic objects. The Wavell collection itself focuses primarily on mid and late twentieth-century creations, which, along with some historical and archaeological material, reflect early traditional designs, allowing us to see how, throughout the century, craft styles evolved in response to historical and market influences.

The far-flung nations of Micronesia, with their relatively small populations, have always produced a modest output of handicrafts. And, as social and cultural anthropologist Adrienne Kaeppler has pointed out, "Micronesia must lead the world in the lack of outside attention given to its traditional and contemporary arts" (Kaeppler et al. 1997:135). Micronesian art has been overlooked by museums, collectors, and publishers alike. Books on Oceanic art generally relegate very little coverage to Micronesia. Perhaps the only large-scale exhibition of Micronesian art held during the twentieth century was held at the University of Hawai'i in 1986 (Feldman and Rubinstein 1986). Other exhibits of Oceanic art have generally featured only a limited number of Micronesian objects. The only real exception to this dearth of coverage occurs in European museums, especially those in

FIGURE 4

9

Germany, where extensive collections acquired during the German period of colonial rule (1899–1919) are housed. Early examples of Micronesian art are somewhat scarce in the U.S., and museums that do possess collections have comparatively minimal public exhibits.

Despite this lack of outside attention, cultural traditions have remained strong on many islands throughout Micronesia. Micronesian peoples have retained their craft skills and, to this day, continue to produce high quality handicrafts. The creative production of tools, baskets, fans, and other culturally unique objects has provided a valuable source of income to remote islands where often the major cash crop is copra—dried coconut meat from which oil is extracted. The production of these handicrafts has also functioned to perpetuate distinctive traditions in the face of western technology. Traditional objects may be crafted with hand-made tools or laboriously prepared with natural materials (as in mat or lava lava weaving and fan or basket production). The quality and detail of these objects often remains high, and, while new materials have been introduced and some styles have changed, Micronesian handicraft production remains a triumph of quality and diversity. Each carefully made object is unique, and it is sometimes possible to identify individual artists or artisans through the distinctive characteristics of their work.

Micronesian art has been praised for its elegance of form. Many utilitarian objects such as tackle boxes and bowls, especially those produced on smaller islands such as those between Yap and Chuuk, are characterized by smooth, sculptural, simplistic lines. Decorative elements, even when very detailed, such as those found on tattoos and mats, often illustrate elaborate geometric patterns. Bowls and other wooden ware can be found with mother-of-pearl inlay. Palau is famous for the architectural splendor of its meetinghouses, which are ornamented with carved and painted designs. Additionally, throughout much of Micronesia, figural sculpture, while often having a squared-off, geometric aspect, is produced in distinctive styles with details including tattoos, clothing, spears, purses, combs, and other accessories.

FIGURE 5

Enthusiastic traders, Micronesian peoples were eager to maximize the scarce resources of their islands. For them, trading has long been an important tradition. They have continually adapted cultural elements to develop desirable items for exchange. Living on many of nearly 2,000 islands in the middle of the Central Pacific, these culturally diverse, unique peoples developed during periods of isolation alternating with moments of intense contact and commerce. Micronesia was settled as early as 1500 B.C., initially probably through drift voyages from the Philippines and from islands in Southeast Asia. Smaller islands maintained tribute relationships with larger islands. Larger islands had more stable and diversified ecosystems. Plus, their resources were less affected by droughts and hurricanes, thus providing outer islanders, traveling on their sophisticated outrigger canoes, a refuge in times of emergency (Alkire 1989:2). Special trade items were developed for these exchanges between larger and smaller islands. Much later, canoes streamed out to greet the occasional European ship, eager to exchange food and crafts for trade goods such as metal tools. From the very beginning, many of their trade objects were items woven by women in a process that has continued to this day, providing women with a strategic basis for economic power and influence.

The earliest Micronesian contact with Europeans occurred shortly after the Spaniard Vasco Núñez de Balboa crossed the Pacific Ocean in 1513. Ferdinand Magellan rounded the tip of South America in 1520 and continued into the Pacific Ocean where, in 1521, he encountered his first Micronesian peoples, the inhabitants of Guam and Rota (Luta). Guam soon became a colony of Spain, along with the Philippines. It was a convenient stopping place for Spanish galleons and became an established settlement during the 1700s. In 1855, the Vatican resolved a dispute between Spain and Germany, and most of Micronesia officially became a Spanish colony. Germany eventually purchased Micronesia from Spain in 1899 when the Spanish needed money to make up for the expense of the Spanish-American War. Then, during WWI, Japan occupied Micronesia and, following a 1919 League of Nations Conference, became officially

FIGURE 6

entrusted with the territory. The United States, after defeating Japan in WWII and recognizing the strategic importance of the Micronesian islands, managed Micronesia as a Trust Territory through the Department of the Interior (Hezel and Berg 1984).

This Trust Territory has now been officially disbanded into separate political entities that include the Federated States of Micronesia (FSM) encompassing four states: Yap, Chuuk (Truk), Pohnpei (Ponape), and Kosrae (Kusaie); the Republic of the Marshall Islands (RMI) (the Ratak and Ralik Chains); the Republic of Palau (Belau) (ROP); the Territory of Guam; and the Commonwealth of the Northern Mariana Islands (Saipan, Rota, and Tinian, among others). The new political entities established in Micronesia are freely associated with the United States, with the exception of Guam and the Northern Marianas. The freely associated states (FSM, RMI, and ROP) have access to U.S. federal programs such as the postal service, the Federal Aviation Administration (FAA), the Federal Emergency Management Agency (FEMA), public health and education grants, and ongoing annual federal funds, as well as visa-free entry for citizens into the U.S., in exchange for perpetual U.S. strategic access rights to their islands. They have U.S. zip codes and, even today, can be reached for the price of a regular U.S. postage stamp. Many of these island areas have undergone multiple name changes in the course of their histories. Since they have achieved independence, several have modified the spelling of their names, which can cause some confusion for those who historically recognize them by another name. In 1990, Truk was renamed Chuuk to correct an original European mispronunciation. Pohnpei has revised its name from the earlier Ponape seen on many maps, and Kosrae has become the modern name for Kusaie. Palau is sometimes also referred to using the local word Belau, but Palau will be used for the purposes of this monograph.

The "Caroline Islands" is a term often used to refer to the Micronesian region and refers to a vast, east-west archipelago that includes Palau, Yap, Chuuk, Pohnpei, and Kosrae. At times, it will be convenient to refer to island locations in terms of their geographic positions within this archipelago rather than in terms of the political affiliation of a given island. Palau is considered part of the Western Carolines, as are several islands that are associated with the Republic of Palau including Hatohobei (Tobi), Merir, Pulo Anna, and the Sonsorol Islands (Fana and Sonsorol/Sonsoral). Atolls between Yap and Chuuk are considered the Central Carolines and include Fais, Ngulu, Sorol, Faraulep, Woleai, Ifaluk (Ifalik), Olimarao, Elato, Gaferut, West Fayu, Pikelot, and Satawal. Chuuk, Kosrae, and Pohnpei are considered part of the Eastern Carolines. The Marshall Islands, which include the Ratak and Ralik Chains, are not to be confused with the Carolines. Kiribati and Tuvalu are two further groups of islands. Formerly known as the Gilbert and Ellice Islands, Kiribati and Tuvalu were British colonies until 1974, and both are now independent nations. Kiribati includes the Gilbert, Phoenix, and Line island groups.

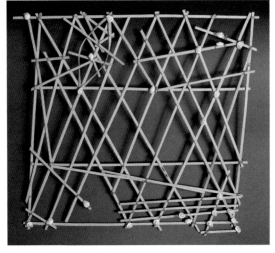

Geographers and anthropologists have divided the Pacific into three major geographic and cultural areas—Polynesia, Melanesia, and Micronesia—for the purpose of understanding the diversity within them. The word Micronesia means "tiny islands." Amazingly, the land area for more than 2,000 individual islands totals no more than 1,000 square miles. Guam is the largest Micronesian island at 225 square miles. In contrast, many atolls are less than a quarter of a square mile in size. While many of the islands are atolls, a few are high islands of sedimentary or volcanic origin (Karolle 1988). The area called Micronesia is situated with Melanesia to the southwest, the Philippines and Southeast Asia to the west, and Polynesia to the east. Based on linguistic studies of the twenty Micronesian languages, Micronesia is thought to have been originally populated from Southeast Asia (Jackson and Marck 1991). However, the blend of physical characteristics of the Micronesians shows the influence of Polynesian and Melanesian migrations.

Despite its dazzling number of island groups, when it comes to the study of Oceanic art, Micronesia is an area that has received short shrift. Perhaps because Micronesia has been colonized longer than any other area of the Pacific, experts in the field have sometimes considered Micronesian material culture to have been contaminated by western contact. In contrast, many New Guinea tribesmen never saw a westerner until WWII forced them to interact. Thus, a Melanesian art object can be considered valuable by outsiders even though it was acquired in the middle of the twentieth century. Polynesia, first encountered in the 1700s by Europeans like Captain James Cook, has produced some of the most striking and coveted examples of Oceanic art collected during this early period, and many books have been devoted to this subject. Thus, overall, material collected from Polynesia prior to 1850 is considered the most valuable, since Europeans had charted most of the islands by that time.

However, in spite of the early Spanish colonization of Guam, many other Micronesian islands continued to have only sporadic contact with the outside world, and this isolation helped to retain early ways of life in many areas. While only a few traditional crafts are found on Guam today, small atolls as well as high islands, such as Yap, Pohnpei, Kosrae, Palau, and the Marshall Islands, have managed to retain active craft traditions. Colonial history continues to play a role, as well. For example, in the Marshall Islands, the Japanese organized handicraft production for economic activity and export. As a result, vestiges of early cultures and belief systems are maintained and perpetuated, sometimes in new and unfamiliar forms. Early missionary activity often tended to discourage art forms, such as figural sculpture, related to traditional religious beliefs. However, neutral pursuits, such as basket and fan making, have been less affected. Today, carved bowls are often replaced by convenient modern substitutes such as ceramic or plastic dishes. Ironically, however, the influx of tourists seeking an "exotic" experience with an "authentic" culture has helped to preserve traditional craft skills by providing economic incentive.

Micronesian handicrafts can still be found on the secondary market that date back to the early post-WWII period when military personnel occupying Micronesian islands such as Palau or Yap collected souvenirs. In addition, beautiful handicrafts are still made today for tourists from

FIGURE 9

14

around the world. Micronesia is especially popular with visitors from Japan and Taiwan, who visit Micronesia to enjoy the tropical scenery and scuba dive, among other activities. American military bases continue to exist throughout Micronesia, including on Guam and in the Marshall Islands. Their military personnel provide a steady market for craft production. In Palau, some art traditions, such as the storyboard, have remained strong. In other areas, such as the Marshall Islands, basket making and weaving skills predominate.

One way of evaluating the age of a craft object from Micronesia is to evaluate changes in the style and use of materials that have occurred over the last sixty years. While some fans created on Kosrae during the 1990s, for example, are virtually identical to those produced nearly one hundred years ago, only older women are continuing to create them. This labor-intensive skill is not being effectively passed on to younger weavers.[1] While some skills such as fan making are at risk of, eventually, being completely lost, other crafts go through a process of evolution as they respond to outside influences, including the introduction of modern technology, modern goods, and a growing market economy. While the use of traditional motifs can serve to affirm cultural identity, art styles may be modified by a number of processes including "simplification," "familiarization," and "material assimilation."

Briefly, "simplification" (Figure 12 and 13) involves the production of items with progressively less detail. As art is mass-produced for profit, less time is spent on individual items, and the more labor-intensive aspects of a process may be compromised or eliminated. Hand fans, which once had tight, finely woven, intricate handles, for example, may now be produced with plainer patterns or coarser weaves. As another example, outrigger canoe models may be less detailed. Fortunately, while tourist art in other areas of the world has often succumbed to this process, Micronesian peoples, largely, continue to produce carefully made, labor-intensive objects.[2] Nevertheless, when comparing two similar objects, the more finely created example is often the older example.

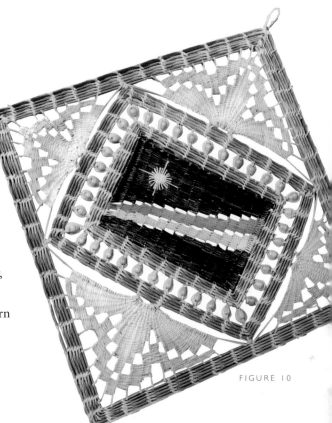

FIGURE 10

15

FIGURE 11

A second process is called "familiarization." This involves the incorporation of traditional motifs into objects familiar to westerners, such as ashtrays, bookends, paper knives, vases, cigarette boxes, or pencil holders. Carved figures can be made into lamps, lighters, or folding bookracks, such as the Palauan example shown in Figure 11. Palauan carvers have adapted themselves well to this process and have even transformed storyboards into coffee tables, which may be sold for several hundred to upwards of one thousand dollars. For those who appreciate tiki kitsch, and even those who just appreciate traditional motifs in a useable object, these items can be skillfully rendered treasures. For those who, like the early German scientific collectors, only value "authentic" items—meaning tools or other objects of cultural value traditionally utilized by Micronesian peoples in daily life—such blended objects may be scorned as culturally polluted.

A third process is called "material assimilation." This process especially applies to woven materials, since the preparation of natural fibers is extremely labor intensive. Material assimilation occurs when non-traditional, imported, or synthetic materials are incorporated into an object. The lava lava, a type of wrap-around skirt traditionally woven on a backstrap loom from banana fibers, is a good example of this process. As cotton thread has become available, islanders first combined it with banana fiber, and now often weave skirts completely from cotton fiber. Another good example is the incorporation of ribbon, yarn, or even strips of plastic into the decoration of fan handles (Figure 130). In fact, yarn and pieces of cloth began to be included into weavings as soon as they became available as trade items. Museum examples with these types of inclusions are seen dating to the early 1900s. Even Yapese lei, once made entirely of natural fibers, are often seen today with the introduction of synthetic fibers into their designs.

The age of an object is most often assessed using a combination of factors. When available, provenance is the most important of these. When and where was the item documented as collected? This information can also help to establish the age and origin for other objects, which appear to be of a similar age and style. However, craft techniques are sometimes adopted and culturally elaborated in areas far from their origin. This process has been occurring long before European cultural contact and is sometimes referred to as "cultural diffusion." Some cultural anthropologists use this process to track associations or contacts between different groups of people. Many factors have facilitated this phenomenon in historical times in Micronesia. Missionaries often came from other areas of the Pacific, such as Samoa or Hawai'i, bringing different fan and basket making traditions with them. Fan designs were also spread from one island to another when islanders were relocated by colonial powers, sometimes in response to droughts or famines or often to meet colonial demands for labor. Another example of the spread of a popular craft item is the storyboard, which originated and developed as a Palauan art form but has now been imitated in Yap and Chuuk. Such occurrences can cause confusion when trying to determine the origin of a craft tradition. A strong example of this is the squatting figure motif. When this style of figure became popularized as a souvenir during the Japanese period of colonial rule, the fact that different atolls produced different styles of the figure became obscured by the fact that the different styles were all marketed on the larger islands of Palau, Guam, and Yap. Carvers from smaller islands often immigrated to larger islands and began producing their own forms of this figure, further confusing the origins of these various carvings.

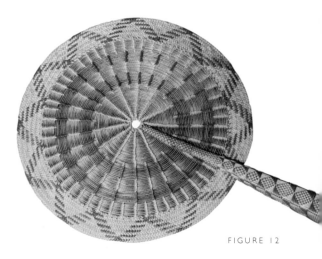

FIGURE 12

FIGURE 13

The area called Micronesia is fascinating. The region's cultures are rich and varied and are still considered exotic by many foreigners. Traditionally, island material culture and artistic production could best be understood in the context of robust traditions of dance and performance. However, in the context of the modern world, many of these performances have become nothing more than entertainment for visitors. Traditional styles and the names of the artists who produced them are rapidly being forgotten as those few who knew them are passing on. This fact especially applies to traditions of figural sculpture. For example, a

FIGURE 15

tradition of Saipanese carving popular during the Japanese period was abandoned during the American occupation and has been rediscovered here only through a process of comparison and deduction. Palauan and Chuukese statuary have been forever changed, as some early traditional features have been largely abandoned, and only Yap continues to produce a very few examples close to the early traditional style. Where figural sculpture can be documented, it provides an important window, not only into pre-western belief systems but also as a way to understand the basic elements of artistic style that defines cultures.

FIGURE 14

FIGURE 16

CHAPTER ONE

Figural Sculpture

Human statuary is a topic about which, perhaps, the most serious misconceptions about Micronesian art have been perpetuated. Most books on Pacific art cover Micronesia in a few sparse pages if at all, while multiple chapters may be devoted to Melanesian and Polynesian art. For example, Maurice Leenhardt's book *Folk Art of Oceania* devotes barely two out of one hundred and twenty-four pages to Micronesia. This minimal coverage also seems to be associated with the belief that Micronesia lacks a significant tradition of figural representation. As Leenhardt states, "The absence of anthropomorphic representation in sculpture has deprived the art of these islands of the most enduring proofs of these people's aesthetics" (Leenhardt 1950:94).

The attitude that Micronesia is lacking in distinctive styles of statuary has then been carried on by later writers. This is despite the fact that Douglas Fraser in his book *Primitive Art* states, "Once thought almost non-existent in Micronesia, figures actually occur in every Micronesian group with the possible exception of the Marshalls" (Fraser 1962:197). Undeniably, the large quantity and diversity of styles found in Melanesia are not present in Micronesia. Additionally, since Micronesian statuary styles evolved on small islands, they were vulnerable to many influences. Environmental disasters, epidemics, and historic interactions with other islands, religions, and cultures have all had a significant influence on carving styles. Despite this vulnerability, however, many figural art styles endured through the twentieth century and are continuing to be produced in varying forms today.

FIGURE 17

21

FIGURE 18

Micronesian statuary can be loosely divided into three categories: standing figures, squatting figures, and weather charms (Figure 4). Standing figures, often found in male/female pairs, once functioned as ancestor figures. Squatting figures may also have originally represented ancestors and, in some cases, fertility. They are also frequently found in pairs. Weather charms, often resembling back-to-back human figures, were hung from canoes to provide protection during dangerous ocean voyages. Instead of legs, they had stingray spines inserted into the torso of the carving and anchored in a mixture of lime. It was difficult to miss weather or navigation charms hanging from outrigger canoes, and this is one category from which the Germans collected many early examples. Weather charms were generally found in the Central Carolines. Other types of early statues in Micronesia may actually have been difficult to spot, since they were sometimes concealed beneath layers of coconut fronds, perhaps as a way of shielding believers from their presumed power. There are many similarities in the treatment of the sacred in Micronesia and Polynesia where "procedures of separating and containing [a sacred object] were important to how divinity was managed," for example the practice of wrapping or binding statues that represented a spirit or ancestor (Hooper 2006:41). In Chuuk and the Central Carolines, coconut fronds were used to delineate sacred spaces and sacred objects such as weather charms, along with other sacred statues. In Palau, statues were kept in household shrines as well as separate dwellings meant just to house and honor spirits.

Early statues were almost always carved of soft woods like breadfruit wood, since, before Micronesian peoples had access to metal carving tools, only shell was available for adze blades on most islands. In Yap, Palau, and the Mortlock Islands (a group of islands in Chuuk, FSM), features like hair, loincloths, and tattoo patterns were sometimes painted on in red (turmeric), black (soot), and white (coral lime), all natural pigments available in Micronesia. In addition, statues are often seen decorated with grass skirts or with strips of palm leaves tied to their arms or legs, similar to the fronds that Micronesian peoples use to ornament themselves for dances or to identify a god.

Styles of figural sculpture have undergone unique transformations in different areas of Micronesia. Nukuoro Atoll, part of Pohnpei State, FSM, is considered the origin of the *tino* image. The *tino* is a simplified figure that is arguably one of the most famous examples of Micronesian statuary, despite the fact that the inhabitants of Nukuoro are thought to have originally have come from Polynesia. Today, similar, smaller *tino* images continue to be carved for the tourist trade, albeit often on Pohnpei itself instead of Nukuoro. Most carvings on Pohnpei are created by carvers from Kapingamarangi Village, a village inhabited by people who migrated to Pohnpei from Kapingamarangi Atoll but who are also considered of Polynesian origin. Most commonly, their carvings depict fish, turtles, and other sea life. While Pohnpei itself produces no documented traditional style of figural sculpture, it is known for one unique example of genre carving depicting a traditional scene in which two men are shown twisting *sakau* roots to produce *kava* (Figure 19). Genre carvings can be defined as carvings that depict activities drawn from everyday life. While male/female figure pairs are the most common form of figural sculpture found in Micronesia, many carvers also produce distinctive genre carvings focusing on characteristic cultural scenes, such as men making *kava*, a woman holding a baby, or a man pounding *poi*.

FIGURE 19

During the twentieth century, many other sculptural styles either are no longer being continued or have changed significantly. Caroline Island carving in Saipan has been discontinued entirely, probably since the early 1960s, while Chuukese sculptures appear to have undergone a sudden change in style at about the same time. A traditional carving style originating on Kuttu in the Mortlock Islands and also produced on Fefan in Chuuk,[3] appears to have been abandoned. Palauan carvings, now largely carved in hardwood, continue to retain some traditional stylistic features, while the statue pairs still produced in Yap remained essentially unchanged through the first half of the twentieth century. Significantly, the stance of both Yapese and Chuukese figures is similar to that of the Nukuoro *tino* images—the arms are at the sides with pointed hands carved free from the hips (or sometimes attached), the feet often not detailed, with the ankles imbedded in the pedestal. Unlike the *tinos*, however, Yapese and Chuukese figures usually had hair and facial features painted on, sometimes with costumes and accessories added. Only in Nukuoro and the Mortlocks, and perhaps on Hatohobei (Tobi), did Micronesians produce large figural sculptures, which were abandoned after western contact (Christian 1899b:170).

YAPESE STATUARY

Yap State is one of the four states that are part of the Federated States of Micronesia. Yap itself consists of five closely grouped islands that are part of "a single, triangularly-shaped submarine platform…surrounded by a fringing reef" (Karolle 1988:96–97). Yap covers only forty-six square miles (Karolle 1988:5) and had a population of 11,241 as of the 2000 census (*FSM* 2002). Yap State also encompasses sixteen outlying islands, including Ulithi, Ngulu, Lamotrek, and Woleai. Yap is considered an important communication center, a principle cable station and important radio transmitting point in the Western Pacific. However, Yap is perhaps most famous for its stone money—the largest and heaviest money found anywhere in the world (Figure 20).

FIGURE 20

The Yapese are recognized to be among the most culturally conservative in Micronesia, and, indeed, examples of Yapese carvings have remained very much the same from the late nineteenth through the mid twentieth centuries. Today, Yapese standing figures in male/female pairs are still sometimes carved of light-colored wood. However, the finest examples of this style usually date from the late nineteenth century through the 1960s (Treide 1997: plates 14, 15). Grass skirts and loincloths were added to these statues, along with traditional tattoos, and hair and facial details were often painted on. Verna Curtis, an individual who, with her husband, helped start and operate craft co-ops in Yap and Chuuk beginning in 1951, advised that only certain individuals from specific family groups or of specific social status were permitted to carve a given design of figure.[4] Certain types or designs of carving were, therefore, considered a form of intellectual property. Such standing figures from Yap were collected extensively during the German period and are found in many museum collections throughout the world today.

Anthropology professor and artist Marvin Montvel-Cohen made observations in Yap over a period of fifteen years starting in 1968 and culminating in his doctoral thesis, which he completed in 1984. He described the Yapese belief in a category of tree spirit called a *doocheraa*. This spirit is found in all wooden objects altered or transformed by human hands and becomes angry when objects are poorly constructed or not treated with proper respect (Montvel-Cohen 1982:117). This belief results in a conservative attitude toward the production of traditional objects since innovation could potentially anger this type of spirit. Ghosts and spirits were believed to inhabit many things, including trees and plants, while ancestral spirits were divided into at least four categories including souls or images, recently dead relatives, long deceased ancestors, and women who had died in childbirth.

FIGURE 21

Montvel-Cohen learned the legend of the *lios*, likely a cognate of the Spanish word "dios" meaning god, from his friend Gilfalan, who was a *salaap* or master carver. The story describes the first carving representing a human who was magically brought to life by the sky gods (Montvel-Cohen 1982:125–129). One of the gods carved the image of a new woman after he became angry with his wife for stealing food. His father then sent his son's wife away and magically brought to life the wooden image of the new wife that his son had carved. Later, the son's original wife returned, and that is how he came to have two wives. This story is chiefly of interest not because it appears to justify polygamy but because it provides a mythological origin for figural representation.

In his ability to make the seemingly magical transformation of a natural object, such as a piece of wood, into an object with cultural meaning and purpose, a *salaap* was considered a skilled mediator between nature and culture (Montvel-Cohen 1982:134). Montvel-Cohen made many visits to Yap to work and live with Gilfalan between 1968 and 1978. He found

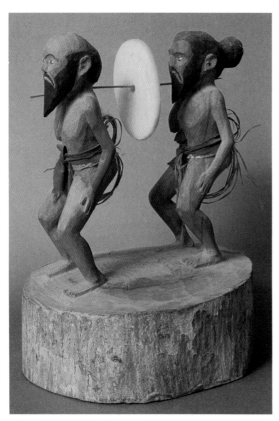

FIGURE 22

Gilfalan to be a spiritual person convinced of the power of spirits and the efficacy of magic (Montvel-Cohen 1982:138). Gilfalan was considered a master carver of house posts, and he refurbished the carvings on old meeting houses. He also carved model Yapese outrigger canoes, made window latches (particularly in the forms of kneeling human figures or pouncing cats), and created other animal wooden carvings. His genre figures included "figures of men and women grinding betel nut or preparing breadfruit, a standing warrior with appropriate *yol*-style tattoo configuration and a row of men performing a movement from a sitting dance" (Montvel-Cohen 1982:139). These figures were usually carved from a log of breadfruit wood, like in the example illustrated in Figure 22 of two men carrying money. Born in the early 1900s, Gilfalan received three years of schooling during his early teens under Japanese rule (Montvel-Cohen 1982:140). He first carved human figures when staying in Colonia, the capital of Yap, while his father was being treated at the Japanese hospital there. He began to explore and test the magical incantations, which were a prelude to carving taught to him by his father, who was also a carver. He concentrated on carving the human form, using his own proportions as a guide and reducing them. His knowledge of the supernatural was so respected that he also acted as a personal soothsayer or *tamanbaey* for a politically powerful chief. He was given many gifts for his services. However, he always redistributed them generously, since it was believed that those who accumulate wealth and possessions as a *salaap* would die prematurely (Montvel-Cohen 1982:143). Gilfalan respected the old ways of doing things and, in fact, refused to wear eyeglasses later in his life, lest wearing them undermine the authenticity of his creations. He believed that "the ghosts who guided him would disapprove" of such an outside influence (Montvel-Cohen 1982:143). Gilfalan lived a rich, productive life, dying in his seventies in 1979. He left no apprentice to carry on his unique style of carving.

As can be seen from Montvel-Cohen's account of Gilfalan's life and beliefs, a carver's artistic production in Yapese society was often intimately associated with his belief in ghosts. Though model outriggers and figures may still be produced today, they are not carved in quite the same ritual and socio-religious context. Nevertheless, Montvel-Cohen's detailed description of Yapese beliefs, and how they constituted an integral part of the production of craft products as recently as the 1970s, shows that twentieth-century craft production, far from being completely adulterated by colonial influence, can still embody significant cultural meaning. A statue of a Yapese man carved in 2001 was obtained through the Yap Art Studio and Gallery. The hair and beard were not painted and the unfamiliar light-colored wood with dark inclusions was polished to a high gloss. However, there was an unmistakable similarity between the shape of the face, with its pointed beard, and the traditional figures that were carved by Gilfalan. The statue was carved by James S. Ungin from Galan, Ramung (a village and island of Yap). An older man, he was reported to be related to Gilfalan, who was from Warilee, Maap (another village and island of Yap), although it is not clear exactly how.[5] This reported connection reinforces Verna Curtis's suggestion that the right to use certain stylistic features in carvings is passed on within families.

Traditional standing figures were also produced on outer islands such as Ulithi or Ngulu and sold in Colonia on the island of Yap. One very old male/female pair, showing traditional yol tattoos indicative of high social ranking (Figure 23), is very similar to a pair documented in the Smithsonian Institution as coming from Ngulu (catalog numbers E387342 and E387343) although their female figure is lacking a skirt. Women wore grass skirts on Ngulu as they do on Yap, so provenance can be especially confusing, although Hera Ware Owen, one of the founding members of the Belau National Museum, suggests that these carvings could have been produced by Judge Joseph Fanechoor.[6] Fanechoor acted as Chief Justice of the District Court in Yap during the early Trust Territory period. A high chief, he was also rumored to be a powerful "magician," no longer welcome in his native Ulithi where he was believed to have caused a typhoon. Like another Ulithi carver, Guar, he claimed to have met David Dean O'Keefe, a successful Irish copra merchant based in Yap. Phillip and Pauline Toomin, in their book *Black Robe and Grass*

FIGURE 23

27

FIGURE 24

FIGURE 25

Skirt, described Fanechoor as "generous with folklore and native craft" (Toomin 1963:191).

Another group of outer-island figures (Figure 24) collected around the late 1950s to early 1960s by a U.S. Naval officer on Ulithi was almost certainly made by the carver Guar, who lived on the Ulithi islet of Faralop. Examples of Guar's figures with red cloths tied to the arms and other distinctive details, including red circular spots painted on the cheeks to represent turmeric dance decorations, are found in the Field Museum in Illinois, the Burke Museum in Seattle, the Bishop Museum in Hawai'i, the Fowler Museum at U.C.L.A, the Museum of Natural History and Planetarium in Rhode Island, and the Peabody Essex Museum in Massachusetts. According to a notation on a Peabody Essex Museum catalog card, "Guar is tattooed with German era motifs and was alive during the Spanish administration and served with O'Keefe."

O'Keefe was a colorful figure in Yapese history. He was a trader born in Ireland who married a woman from Savannah, Georgia. He helped the Yapese quarry stone money from Palau, providing his ship for transport in exchange for labor and copra. O'Keefe was active in Micronesia from approximately 1871 to 1901 when he disappeared at sea. This fact leads us to conclude that Guar was young when he met O'Keefe (Klingman and Green 1950). Guar appears to have died by the early 1970s. Figure 25, a photograph taken in 1950, shows an older Guar carving one of his statues while a young boy looks on. Referred to as "Huar" in Fowler Museum records, Guar was said to have carved his statues with steel adzes and other tools obtained from German traders. A "doll," with essentially identical stylistic features, also at the Peabody Essex Museum, however, was listed as having come from Fais, a nearby atoll, and not Ulithi. When people donate their carvings to museums, their memory may not always be accurate. They often remember where they bought the object but not necessarily where it was said to have originated. This is why it is a good idea when researching museum records, to view as many documented examples of a carving style as possible. According to the Peabody Essex Museum, Guar was the only carver of such "dolls" in Ulithi. However, while Guar was undoubtedly the only carver of such "dolls" on the Ulithi islet of Faralop, another carver, Ululimar,[7] carved pairs of figures on another islet, Asor, at least until the late 1960s or early 1970s. Any Ulithi-style figure not done in Guar's distinctive style could be considered for attribution to Ululimar as, in general, slight but distinctive differences in the style of a sculpture, especially in facial features, are indications of the work of a different carver. A third carver of this style of tattooed, male figure is documented by Edwin Grant Burrows, who did research on Ifaluk in 1948 and 1953 (Burrows 1963:17). He illustrates a carved standing figure of a man with tattoos, which he documents as carved and painted by Gabwileisei. The statue has a distinctive face with an aquiline nose but is otherwise quite similar to those of Guar and Ululimar. All three of these carvers have depicted male figures with the characteristic style of *yol* tattoos, indicative of high status, covering their chests. One contemporary Yapese carver, Rudolf Ken (Figure 26), creates male and female standing figures in his own unique version of this style. The male figure he has carved illustrates the *zalbachag* style of tattooing in which the legs are covered with geometric markings. This style of tattoo, also indigenous to Yap, was worn by men who were successful warriors. A third form of tattoo called *gachow* is variable in form and can be worn by men or women. Female statues can sometimes be seen with *gachow* tattoos as well, such as a row of paired dolphins along the sides of the thighs (Untaman & Whitcomb 1956:72–73). Yapese and Yapese outer-island sculptures continue to be among the most culturally authentic, since their production has resisted outside influences more effectively than any other island group.

FIGURE 26

Chuuk State is another of the four states that make up the Federated States of Micronesia. It consists of fifty-five volcanic islands surrounded by atolls, reefs, and many islets, and it covers only thirty-nine square miles of land (Karolle 1988). Chuuk is comprised of several island groups including the Mortlock and the Hall Islands. As of the 2000 census, Chuuk had a population of 53,595 (*FSM* 2002). During WWII, the islands of Chuuk provided a strategic location for the Japanese fleet because of its large, deep lagoon, which can harbor many ships. Today, beneath its waters, the wrecks of Japanese vessels sunk by American bombers are a popular scuba diving destination for Chuuk's visitors.

The Mortlock Islands, a small group of islands in Chuuk State, FSM, are famous for the black and white *tapuanu* masks that American co-op organizer Verna Curtis described as "like a Jack of Cards" in their appearance (Figure 27). The word *tapuanu* means "sacred soul or spirit" and refers to the carved wooden masks worn by Chuukese men during ceremonial dances. It also refers to *tapuanu* idols, which are carved standing figures representing male and female figures wearing the masks. The large masks, the only documented masks found in Micronesia, were worn in a dance ceremony performed to "battle with the wind," thereby protecting crops such as breadfruit and taro from the damage of typhoons (Kaeppler et al. 1997:197–201). Similar smaller masks were hung as gable decorations, and this type was later often sold to tourists due to their more portable size. Physician and anthropologist Augustin Krämer illustrates one example of a *tapuanu* figure with small hands, small uneven feet, and a relatively large head inclined slightly upwards (Krämer 1935:118). Another pair of figures, shown here and now in a private collection, are rare examples of Mortlock standing figures actually wearing the *tapuanu* masks (Figure 28). They were said to have been obtained through European dealers at the beginning of the twentieth century.

Since the word *anu* means god or spirit, *tapuanu* figures may have been intended to portray ancestors in their role as guardians. Unfortunately, no detailed account is available as to how these figures were actually

FIGURE 27

used, though we know that the masks themselves were worn by male clan members who performed songs and dances having ritual or magical significance. However, Max Girschner, government physician during the German period, observed that, in the Mortlocks, ancestors, especially recently deceased chiefs or heroes, could attain the status of *anu* and become guardian spirits for their clans. One such guardian spirit from Namoluk in the upper Mortlocks was carved from a block of breadfruit wood and decorated with a necklace and girdle. It could be found sitting in a large canoe in a clubhouse there. The statue was presented with offerings, and permission had to be asked before he could be removed from the canoe to allow the men to use it. The people revered but also feared this image since, if he were angered, it was thought that he could send storms or sickness (Girschner 1911:192). The *tapuanu* figures may also have been revered and given offerings in exchange for protecting crops. However, since the figures, as well as the masks, generally came in male/female pairs, they may also have symbolized fertility or an appeal to an all-powerful god, rather than a specific ancestor.

FIGURE 28

Occasionally, male and female figures without the masks show up in the art market. One French dealer and author, Jean-Edouard Carlier, illustrates what is probably such a figure in his catalog *Micronesie et Para-Micronésie* (Carlier 2007:125). He identifies the female figure as Palauan, but Carlier's example clearly has ear spools, as do most early statues in this characteristic style. While Palauans and Yapese did not wear ear spools, many islanders in the Central Carolines enlarged their lobes and/or wore elaborate earrings or ear spools. We also know from illustrations in Otto von Kotzebue's voyages (1815–1818 and 1823–1826) that Marshall Islanders who are not known to have produced figural sculpture also wore ear spools or, more accurately, ear bundles or cylinders that stuck out on either side of their ear lobes. The males wore larger ear bundles than the females. Several island groups associated with Chuuk, including the Mortlock Islands, Houk, Satawal, and Puluwat, certainly wore ear spools. In addition, at least one group on Kuttu Island, one of islands in the Mortlocks, portrayed them on their statuary. An assortment of ear

FIGURE 29

31

FIGURE 30

spools from Houk, Satawal, and Puluwat is illustrated in Damm and Sarfert's publication (Damm and Sarfert 1935:38–39). The ear spool is thought to have spread from the Mortlocks to other island groups, and certain ear spool decorations were typically worn by women and young girls at dances. Kotzebue's companion from Woleai had elongated ear lobes, but an early photo of a man from Ulithi shows only a small piercing designed to hold flowers, so this custom probably did not spread as far as Ulithi (Hezel and Berg 1984:64, 100–101). One of the few English references to Mortlock statuary is a 1949 Trust Territory pamphlet on Micronesian Crafts produced by the U.S. Division of Education, which briefly refers to Kuttu dolls from Chuuk. While acting as postmistress on Chuuk between 1950 and 1957, Frankie Teel Mayo collected such a pair of figures (Figure 29) with ear spools on the islet of Kuttu.[8] A back-to-back figure (Figure 30), along with a mother-and-child figure (Figure 32), have also been collected, showing that this style was expanded to depict genre figures. The portrayal of ear spools on Kuttu statues was increasingly abandoned after the 1950s, and no statues in traditional Kuttu style have so far been found with established provenance after the late 1960s or early 1970s.

Instead of ear spools, some Chuukese standing statues are portrayed wearing heavy, elaborate earrings. Chuuk Islanders are historically recognized as having worn the largest and heaviest earrings of any group in Micronesia (Hezel and Berg 1984:17). The ear lobes of boys and girls were enlarged around the age of twelve by weighting the piercing with "collars" of tortoiseshell[9] and then using progressively larger plugs of pandanus leaves (LeBar 1964:162). In Chuuk Lagoon, earrings generally consisted of many coconut shell rings to which conus shell (cone shell) discs were attached (LeBar 1964:163). These earrings were very heavy, especially on men, and the shell discs often hung down onto their shoulders, giving them a fearsome look. Even in the 1950s, some of the older men and women on Chuuk still had distinctive, enlarged ear lobes (Figures 31 and 95). A catalog entitled "Micronesian Navigators and Their Culture," from an exhibit at the Folk Museum of Ota City in Tokyo

FIGURE 31

in 1997, illustrates a pair of figures attributed to the Mortlock Islands showing the male with heavy hanging ear ornaments consisting of coconut and shell rings. Another such wooden, male figure found in the Smithsonian Institution collection has hanging earrings carved as part of the statue (Cat. # 394984). Figure pairs in the "maskless" *tapuanu* style generally show the female with a carved, often striped skirt or *lava lava*, her hair painted black and hanging down her back or in a squared-off bun. The male wears a loincloth and has his hair in a squared-off bun as well. His hair and beard are usually painted black in a style similar to that seen on Mortlock masks and some weather charms. Early statues may also be partially painted in white, a coloring which is derived from coral lime similar to that used on early Mortlock masks. Sometimes Kuttu figures appear to represent specific people, some examples having a portrait-like aspect.

In many ways, these traditional male/female figure pairs, carved out of light-colored, breadfruit wood seem to mirror those still occasionally produced in Yap. Both types of figures carved from light-colored wood have painted details such as hair, beards, eyes, nipples, and traditional dress. Generally, the Kuttu figures have no tattoos, and the Ulithi figures lack ear spools. During the Japanese period, artist and ethnologist Atsushi Someki stated that he preferred Mortlock Island masks and *mok mok* dolls to the ever-popular Tobi squatting figure. The similar phrase *mog mog* was also used to identify a pair of *tapuanu*-like figures illustrated in "The Hijikata Hisakatsu Exhibit" (Hijikata 1991:142).[10] *Mog mog* is defined in a Caroline-English dictionary as a general phrase describing starch, which sometimes specifically refers to taro or arrowroot. The term *mog mog* may refer to the statue's role similar to that of the masks, in protecting crops from typhoons, for example. However, apart from being a word for starch, Mogmog is also the name of one of the smaller islands of Ulithi in Yap State. Could the use of this term imply some of these statues were carved on Mogmog? This is unlikely, based on the fact that all the objects in the Hijikata Hisakatsu catalog are identified by their native language name and not their place of origin. For example, a Palauan

FIGURE 32

33

FIGURE 33

FIGURE 34

statue is referred to as a *dilukai*, a phrase that initially referred to a female figure over the Palauan *bai* but was later generalized to refer to all Palauan statuary. Further, the Hijikata Hisakatsu statues are wearing square ear spools but, otherwise, are extremely similar to the figure pair documented to have come from Kuttu Island in the Mortlocks. It is even possible that these statues were completed by the same carver or another member of his clan. Early illustrations of men from Ulithi do not appear to portray enlarged ear lobes. Instead, a distinctly different style of carving, which focuses more on tattoo patterns, has been documented in Ulithi.

It is likely that the Kuttu Island style figures spread to Chuuk from the Mortlocks, since figural sculpture was reportedly not common in Chuuk during early times. An informant told anthropologist Ward Goodenough "the only purpose for which carved images were used" was to direct "magic" against a victim in a form of sorcery (Goodenough 2002:268–269). During times of war, dead bodies or carvings depicting the human form were used to focus magic against the enemy. In times of peace, carvings of fish were often used to focus sorcery in a similar way. Most of the evidence supports the contention that Kuttu Island and Kuttu islanders who lived on Moen (one of the main islands of Chuuk) were the primary source of the style of figure. Significant variations on such statues may represent carvers from other islands in the Central Carolines.

According to James Nason, curator emeritus of ethnology at Seattle's Burke Museum and professor of anthropology at the University of Washington in the late 1960s, a Kuttu carver produced a pair of book-ends based on an African initiation mask (from the Bamileke tribal group), which was illustrated on a poster in the Peace Corps office. These carvings were then purchased by Nason on Moen. The mask was copied onto the face of the figure, while the body was improvised by the carver.[11] Such examples illustrate how easily outside influences can affect the production of Chuukese carvers.

Statuary continues to be created today on Chuuk but in quite a different style. The wood used is stained dark brown (usually with shoe polish) but is actually a relatively light-colored, soft wood. Male figures are generally portrayed with top-knots and beards and holding carved spears, fish, or fish nets (Figure 33) or seated and pounding breadfruit (Figure 34). However, the overall body style of contemporary figures is much more sculptural and lacks the geometric stylized feel of the older carvings. Chuuk figural sculpture has continued to evolve, and some early styles are no longer being made.

The Republic of Palau consists of a group of over 200 volcanic islands and islets. Palau covers an area of 192 square miles and had an estimated population of 18,766 in 2000 (Advameg 2010). Palau was the headquarters of the Japanese mandate in Micronesia during the Japanese colonial period. During this time, many Japanese moved to Palau and greatly developed its infrastructure and economy. Today, Palau is a popular tourist destination for divers and is known for its unique architecture.

By January 1871, when John Stanislaw Kubary, a German naturalist and ethnographer, visited Palau, the most common form of figural sculpture were *dilukai* figures used to decorate bai. Though traditionally they were in the form of a woman whose open legs were spread above the doorway of the men's house, Kubary also documented male figures, standing figures, and even one in the image of a sailor. The female *dilukai* figure was generally depicted wearing a piece of bead money around her neck, with her mons, and sometimes the inside of her legs were blackened to represent traditional tattoos. Women of the local village were forbidden to enter through the doors of the *bai* above which the *dilukai* hung. As an explanation for the origin of the *dilukai* figure, Kubary was told the story of a man who went fishing, leaving his two sisters at home. Their village was attacked and the sisters fled, finally finding refuge in the *bai* of another village. This story may also explain the origin of the "*mengol* system." In this system, women known as *mengols* took part in institu-

FIGURE 35

FIGURE 36

tionalized exchanges between villages, earning money and prestige by serving men in the *bai* before ultimately marrying, often, one of the men they served. This practice could involve a group of women offered with the support of their home village, a single woman seeking political advantage, or sometimes a woman taken against her will. As Kubary suggested, "… the [*dilukai*] figure [on the *bai*] symbolizes the concept of riches resulting from the sexual importance of the woman" (Kubary 1889:244).

In reference to religious statuary, Kubary added that "there exist today no more than six wooden idols…made in the past. They were kept in caves and brought out only on the occasion of the *ruk* [a dance]" (Kubary: 1889:248–249). Such statues generally represented gods or ancestors called *chelids*, *galids*, or *kaliths*.[12] They were kept in small shrines that were often miniature, ornate representations of Palauan buildings. This practice, analogous to the use of house shrines found in Indonesia, very likely originated there. Some villages, considering their people to be related through their ancestral spirits, undertook reciprocal visits carrying the *kleangel*, a wooden box thought to hold the spirit of a common ancestor (Parmentier 1987:97). Villages held prestigious *ruk* dances and *mur* feasts, which could go on for days and involved the presentation of valuables. Kubary describes the use of statues in Airai, a state on Babeldaob Island, Palau, in association with a *ruk* by stating the following: "Unique in Palau, very old wooden idols are openly displayed that are otherwise kept in the cavities of a *koheal*. (The *koheal* was apparently a cavity, sometimes in a cliff, where the statues were stored.) One such shrine is constructed at the top of a lofty coconut palm and in this is placed the wooden male figure…and his consort…during the performance of the *ruk*…and every evening they are taken down. After the *ruk* is over, the idols are returned to their cavities…in a high cave on the water side of the limestone cliff" (Kubary 1885:110–111). The adjacent photograph taken by German administrator Georg Fritz in 1905 shows two Palauan women standing (or perhaps dancing) with statues on their heads (Figure 36). Their statues are similar to an example shown in Treide's 1997 publication, *In den Weiten des Pazifik* (Treide 1997:

plate 82). Treide's example was collected in northwest Babeldaob by Karl Semper, a zoologist attached to the University of Würzburg, who spent ten months in Palau. The Fritz photo may show Palauans who had been exiled to the Marianas due to their religious activities on Palau. Fritz was a district officer in Saipan from 1899 to 1907 and mostly wrote about his experiences with the Chamorro on the Mariana Islands. He also compiled a significant collection of photographs, now in the possession of the University of Guam.

During their colonial administration of Palau (1899–1914), German authorities believed that the elaborate feasts, such as the *mur*, and exchanges associated with the *ruk* dances diverted attention from the production of copra and other practical labor. Thus, they outlawed the dances and restricted participation in the clubhouse system, not realizing that it had been a traditional way of recruiting labor. As German missionaries sought to introduce Christianity, and as the system of clubhouses and the exchange of traditional bead money were disrupted by German colonial rule, shrines fell into disuse, and many statues were destroyed or traded. The drop in Palauan population from disease was another factor that made it difficult to maintain traditional practices.

Early Palauan statues, like those of Chuuk and Yap, were carved from light-colored, soft wood such as breadfruit, and details such as hair were, as stated previously, often portrayed in a boxy bun. Sometimes hair and traditional tattoos were painted in black. The unique Palauan grass skirt was also depicted as squared, often with sharp corners. Several examples of nineteenth-century statues can be seen in Treide's book (Treide 1997: plates 76–82).

During the Japanese period, post figures, which could be quite large, were collected. However, Palauan carvers, along with Hatohobeian (Tobian) carvers resident in Palau, seemed to concentrate more on producing the ever popular "Tobi" squatting figures, which, in some cases, incorporated features similar to traditional *dilukai* statuary (Figure 36). Those

FIGURE 37

37

FIGURE 38

standing figures that were produced were sometimes derived from the statuary of post figures, which were used to decorate the *bai*, although standing figures were also traditionally used to decorate bowls.

Examples of Palauan standing figures produced during the American period can be readily identified since they now begin to be carved of hardwoods and often had inlaid eyes of mother-of-pearl, like the squatting figures. Other details, like the traditional boxy hair buns depicted for both males and females and the boxy skirts on female sculptures, continued to be included at first (through the late 1960s), but, later, they adopted a smoother, western sculptural style. Several genre figures were developed, including male head hunters holding a spear and one or more severed heads on a pole, fishermen holding fish and a spear, warriors equipped with spears and clubs, and female figures shown cradling children or holding a basket with one hand, on their head with both hands, or in their laps. Many Palauan figures continued to exhibit traditional stylistic features that reflect the unique Palauan aesthetics of style. In some newer carvings, these figures are sometimes portrayed as similar to the characters portrayed in storyboards. Palauan statuary has always been produced in relatively small quantities, often by the same carvers who produced storyboards. Heinrich was one well-known carver who produced many statues and often, but not always, signed his work.

Another famous storyboard carver, also known for his standing figures, was Osiik (Figure 6). Osiik is most famous for his unique, stylized storyboard figures, which have been compared to the free form figures of French artist Henri Matisse (Kagle 1976:15). Osiik was known as an inventive carver, and his standing figures often had large, distinctive ears, which stuck out on each side. Their bodies were slender and angular, with the requisite skirts, loincloths, baskets, and weapons added. Ngerbehid was another Palauan considered a great carver, but his works are rare since he produced very few examples. He carved figures in light-colored, soft wood, sometimes painted black and exhibiting the stylized sculptural planes of the early Palauan style.

In general, while Palauan standing figures are less traditional and more innovative than Yapese carvings, they are relatively uncommon, since Palauan carvers devote most of their energy to storyboard carving. Zacharius Omengebar was a storyboard artist who sometimes carved pairs of figures. Ling Inabo owns the highly successful Tebang Wood Carving Shop on Koror Island in Palau. One of his carvings (Figure 38) depicts a woman during the First Childbirth Ceremony, a celebration that involves several days of ritual bathing of the mother followed by a gathering where food is provided and gifts are brought for the mother and baby. Another gifted carver who focuses on male and female figure pairs is Lee Pedro of Sonsorol. Although Sonsorol is technically part of Palau, it is culturally more closely related to the islands surrounding Yap. Pedro's figures have skillfully detailed, traditional Sonsorol tattoos inked on, similar to the Yapese and Ulithi figures. While the illustrated pair of figures are classic in form (Figure 39), sometimes his carvings are fanciful and even grotesque. While Palauan wood carving continues to be dominated by storyboard production, there are still many gifted artists who produce statuary.

FIGURE 39

CAROLINE ISLANDS WOOD CARVINGS IN SAIPAN

Caroline Islanders who immigrated to Saipan inspired a distinctive style of figural sculpture that is no longer being produced today. Consisting largely of standing sculptures of men and women, this carving style was elaborated on during the Japanese colonial administration. A period of prolific production of these figures appears to have coincided with Japanese, Carolinian, and Chamorro internments in a civilian camp on Saipan following WWII. Recognition of this unique sculptural tradition has come about largely from the stylistic comparison of this distinctive type of chip carving with other Micronesian carvings, including the Caroline Island figures from which they appear to derive. These carvings were still being produced and were sold to military personnel and administrators as tourist items immediately after the American occupation. However, by the early 1960s, this style of carving appears to have been largely abandoned.

Caroline Islanders from atolls between Yap and Chuuk were trading with the Mariana Islands as early as the 1780s, probably continuing traditional trading patterns that existed prior to European contact. Between 1815 and 1820, the Spanish governor allowed Caroline Islanders to immigrate to the Marianas provided they agreed to use their outriggers and navigational skills to help in distributing messages throughout the islands. Their islands had been struck with devastating typhoons that destroyed their coconut palms and taro patches and resulted in a series of famines. Saipan, originally occupied by native Chamorro, had been evacuated by the Spanish in an effort to consolidate political control during their initial occupation. The earliest permanent settlement of Caroline Islanders is thought to have occurred around 1815 (Butler 1995:15–20). Later, Chamorro settlers from Agana, Guam, and Christianized Carolinians established further settlements. However, unlike most Chamorro who had become acculturated to Spanish ways, the Carolinians continued to live using traditional subsistence techniques and material culture. Even today, they are considered the most traditional among the various populations found on Saipan.

FIGURE 40

An original Saipan carving, the one that initiated this study, was carved from heavy hardwood and depicts a standing woman wearing a grass skirt and presenting an oval dish filled with fruit (Figure 41). Her features are finely detailed, and her head comes to a flattened point behind, to represent her hair in an abstract bun. Her arms are massive and her back deeply grooved. The figure was chip carved, a carving technique in which carving marks are left visible rather than sanded smooth. The grass skirt, characteristic Micronesian bowl shape, and distinctive hardwood, which, from its grain, appeared similar to Palauan *dort* or ironwood (*intsia bijuga*, also known as *ifil* wood in Guam), hinted at an origin somewhere in Micronesia. But, at an Association of Social Anthropologists in Oceania (ASAO) meeting in the early 1990s, none of the attending anthropologists could identify the statue. The consensus was that this carving must be an island figure carved by a European, since no Micronesian carver would express that particular aesthetic.

An article by George Hynd, entitled "*Taotaomona*: A Functional Belief Among the Chamorro People," pointed to Guam as a potential origin for the statue, since it included a photograph of a Guam student's conception of a *taotaomona* carved from coconut wood (Hynd 1975:18). The large, blocky limbs and tiny, detailed facial features of this spirit carving were in a style very reminiscent of the female standing figure, but the similarities were not enough to be conclusive. In retrospect, however, they do seem to confirm that such carvings were still being made in the mid 1970s.

During the late 1990s, the internet began to allow for a systematic search of auction sites and museum collections for Micronesian carvings. Four figures turned up in Hawai'i with stylistic similarities (squatting figures in foreground of Figure 40). Three of these had squatting postures similar to those of the "monkeyman" figures. But, the hands of the male figures rested alongside their buttocks, instead of on their knees. The figures were also carved from a heavy, dark-colored wood similar to *dort*, the same as the original standing figure. The two male figures had red loincloths painted on. Incidentally, red is a preferred color for the loincloths of Caroline Islanders. One female figure had a striped, painted on, red and green skirt, while the other had a red skirt with painted on colored fibers around the waist and flowers painted in her hair. All the figures had painted red lips and crude, chip-carved features. The delineated nipples, large arms, and grooved backs of both of the female figures were very reminiscent of the standing figure originally collected. One female figure was squatting, the other sitting. The sitting figure had her knees drawn up in an awkward way, which matched the stance in a photograph of a Micronesian figure from the collection of the late Leo Fortess. Fortess, a well-known collector of Pacific artifacts, had originally obtained the figure from the estate of William Charlock III, a former Trust Territory administrator. While the skirts, loincloths, and stylistic features were all evocative of Caroline Islanders' traditional dress, these similarities were still not conclusive.

FIGURE 41

FIGURE 42

Next, a pair of male and female figures (twelve inches and twelve and one-half inches high) were located in California (back right in Figure 40). Both figures again were chip carved from dark-colored hardwood. The female had a carved-on grass skirt and, like the original figure, was holding a bowl that appeared to be filled with fruit and was in the same posture as the original statue. The male figure had a carved-on loincloth, and, in short, they both belonged to the same stylistic tradition as those already discussed. However, proof that is more conclusive came along in the form of another female figure in what was, by now, clearly a popular genre pose—holding a bowl of fruit in front of her body, bare breasted, with a carved-on skirt. She was standing on a large block of wood, probably originally designed to function as a bookend, with "Saipan" incised on the base. This characteristic pose of a grass-skirted woman holding a bowl of fruit is exemplified in five of the fourteen figures, which have so far been acquired in this style, including the most recent acquisition that has "Saipan 1947" carved on it.

The fact that all of the figures described so far have been chip carved may constitute a clue to their syncretic origins, since both Germans and Japanese have chip-carving traditions. Chip carving is practiced among the Ainu, an ethnic group in the north of Japan, and is also a characteristic of German folk carvings. While few written references to Saipan carvings can be found, a 1949 pamphlet produced by the Trust Territory Division of Education entitled "Arts and Crafts of the Trust Territory of the Pacific Islands" describes a Saipan carving tradition. "Wooden figures carved from tanuki wood are a Japanese craft in Saipan, as also are the lady dolls of wood and cloth" (Anonymous 1949:18). A "lady doll" consists of a detailed head and a body dressed in cloth, which is usually mounted on a wooden stick. An example of a wooden female figure holding a bowl of fruit before her, similar to Figure 42, can be seen on display in the Commonwealth of the Northern Mariana Islands Museum. According to this museum's online narrative, this style of statue was being produced by Caroline Islanders in internment camps, where they were confined from July of 1944 through July of 1946. As one quote from the site explained, "They wanted to teach the kids about their past, so they built a place to do their arts and crafts, to make a living out of it, and to do something worthwhile inside the internment camps…. There are carvings from Carolinians depicting their place in Yap and in Palau" (*Pacific Worlds & Associates 2004*).

However, according to a report by then-Lieutenant Commander Dorothy Richard, produced for the U.S. Navy on the war-time military government of the Trust Territory, Japanese and Chamorro also played a significant role in handicraft production (Richard 1957). After WWII, Japanese, Chamorro, Carolinians, and Koreans were placed in Camp Susupe, a civilian internment camp on Saipan in the Northern Mariana Islands. There, the Naval Administration attempted to differentiate friend from foe and decide whether to allow individuals to remain in Saipan or to return them to their countries of origin. Of 17,974 civilian residents of Camp Susupe in April of 1945, only 810 were Carolinian, while over 13,000 were Japanese, 1365 were Korean, and 2426 were Chamorro. However, Carolinians were not always identified separately from Chamorro in statistical studies, perhaps since the two groups shared housing in the camp while Japanese and Koreans were housed separately. A daily labor report for July 1945 mentions Carolinians in the introduction but does not separate them out from the Chamorro on the actual graph (Richard 1957:508). In fact, a number of statistical studies appear to lump the Chamorro and Carolinians together as "Chamorro." Similarly, the handicraft project at Camp Susupe recorded as beginning in July 1944 identified sixty-eight Japanese and sixty-one Chamorro handicraft workers who were soon producing twenty-three items a week (Richard 1957:10). Although Carolinians were not specifically mentioned in the report, at least a percentage of the handicraft workers listed as "Chamorro" must have been Carolinian due to the culturally correct material they produced. The carvings themselves reflect a familiarity with the Carolinian ethos that appears to go beyond imitation, and reproduces many features of Carolinian statues produced on Yap and Chuuk and the atolls in between, including occasional awkwardness in the portrayal of

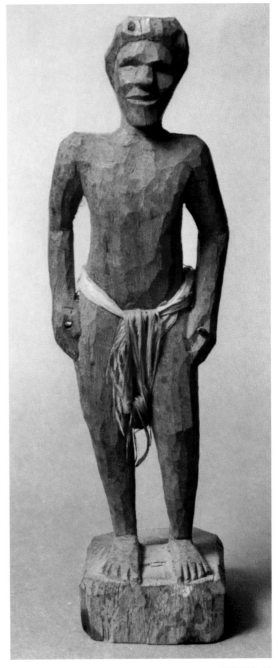

FIGURE 43

43

female legs (especially in seated subjects), pointed hair buns, and Carolinian clothing styles. Specific carvings even seem reminiscent of specific carvers from Yap or surrounding outer islands. For example, the two tallest figures shown in Figure 40 have features similar to the facial features seen on Gilfalan's figure pairs.

Unfortunately, no detailed account exists to tell us the exact nature of the collaboration between different carvers in Camp Susupe or to allow us to know for certain whether any of them were Carolinian. Richard provides a photograph of a selection of Micronesian handicrafts including many that were undoubtedly produced on Camp Susupe (Richard 1957:268). Some of them are typical products of the Caroline Islands, such as *lava lava* and Chuukese-style clubs. Swagger sticks, standing figures, and a squatting figure portrayed next to a coconut bowl (similar to Figure 44) all epitomize the chip-carved style (Richard 1957:510). But, the great majority of handicrafts listed in Richard's report, including baskets, cigarette cases, handbags, belts, and hats, would have been produced by women. In fact, of all the women registered to work in Camp Susupe, fifteen percent were handicraft workers. The only two slightly larger categories of employment for women were those of farm workers and common laborers. Only a half of a percent of all men registered to work were employed as handicraft workers, suggesting that these specific men may have had some special interest or specialized knowledge (Richard 1957:504). Model canoes and swagger sticks would have been produced by the men along with some components of "dolls." "Dolls" was a term that was not defined by Richard but probably included "lady dolls," as well as other categories of figural sculpture. Significantly, a second civilian internment camp, Camp Churo, established on Tinian (also in the Northern Marianas) was occupied primarily by Japanese and Koreans, along with a small number of Chinese. The twenty-six Chamorro found there were sent back to Camp Susupe on Saipan (Richard 1957:554–555). Individuals in this second camp also produced handicrafts such as woven shoes, cigarette cases, handbags, tablemats, hats, bracelets, and coasters. However, without any workers listed as "Chamorro," they produced

FIGURE 44

FIGURE 45

generic woven items without any obvious Micronesian association
(Richard 1957:589). No outrigger canoes, clubs, or "dolls" were
produced, undermining the argument that any of these categories of
particular crafts were of Japanese origin. One serviceman, present when
the Caroline Islanders were released from internment in 1946, received
a Chuukese-style club (Figure 47) and a swagger stick to commemo-
rate the event. This style of swagger stick, which essentially has a small,
chip-carved, female figure at the top, is illustrated by Dorothy Richard
(Richard 1957:268). The serviceman's Chuukese-style club, currently
in the Wavell collection, is also identical to those shown in Richard's
illustration and has "Saipan 1946" carved on the side. Photographs from
the estate of Irwin Kile Vandam, a Commander in the U.S. Navy who was
responsible for establishing a school system throughout the Trust Territory from 1948 to 1950, illustrate one of the crafts fairs held after Camp
Susupe closed. The chip-carved style can also be seen there among other
handicraft items depicted in the photograph.

In short, based on the evidence presented above, it appears unlikely
that the chip-carved style was a fabrication of Japanese artisans under
the watchful eye of American soldiers. There is evidence that Caroline
Islanders may have been producing this realistic style of carving for over
a century. The Krämer Expedition, a German expedition conducted in

the early 1900s to study the islands of Micronesia, encountered a unique tackle box on Lamotrek Atoll with figural carvings. "This curious item is a box, embellished with Greek figures, a seated figure [of a woman] on the broad sides, and a standing figure [of a woman] on the ends. A Spaniard, Gulio, who arrived on Lamotrek at the time of the typhoon of 1907, may have been responsible for carving this box" (Krämer, 1937:64). The standing woman is plump and without apparent clothing, while the seated woman has her hair painted black and appears to be wearing a skirt, based on the illustration of the box (Krämer 1937:64). Thus, as early as 1907, an object was collected decorated with figural sculpture, which the Germans interpreted as being European in style. Similarly, the anthropologists who viewed the standing figure brought to the Association of Social Anthropologists in Oceania (ASAO) meeting reacted with suspicion. Did these carvings in an unexpectedly realistic chip-carved style truly represent "traditional" Micronesian artistic production? Certainly, the idea that European sailors with carving skills may have influenced the carving styles of Caroline Islanders cannot be ignored. Nor can we ignore the possibility that Japanese souvenir needs contributed to Carolinian carving production, since this figural style appeared to be already well established on Saipan shortly after WWII. On the other hand, we have already described examples of realistically carved standing figures that were being extensively collected in Yap and Chuuk during this period and were considered traditional. Such statues differ from Saipan carvings in significant ways. They were carved of light-colored rather than dark-colored wood and were often painted with individually made accessories. Both types are, nevertheless, more similar than different in overall style.

Changes or departures from what is perceived as an early "traditional" style may undermine the value of an object being offered for sale. However, our western need to recognize only early, unchanged forms of material culture has undoubtedly resulted in a significant loss of information, since transitional objects and innovations may tell us a great deal about historical and artistic influences. Fortunately, tourists are

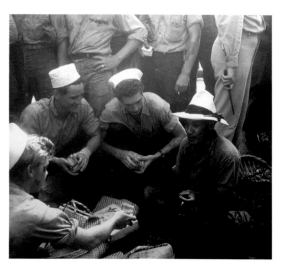

FIGURE 46

usually less aware of issues of cultural authenticity, although the choices they make can influence the subsequent production of objects in other ways. For example, tourists often prefer objects that are small and portable. Most are also attracted to traditional styles, which have been modified for western use (familiarization). The chip-carving tradition in Saipan provided such objects in the form of swagger sticks, ashtrays, and bookends. However, in the final analysis, no matter which objects of material culture are collected or selected, we are influencing both the producers of the art themselves, as well as our own understanding of the significance of the product. Nevertheless, the attribution of this figural style as a form of "Japanese craft" may have served to usher in its demise, since the early post-WWII period was characterized by a rejection of Japanese influence. Perhaps, as Richard suggests, handicraft production on Saipan was actually largely abandoned simply because more reliable forms of wage labor gained precedence after U.S. troops left and most of the Japanese had been returned home.

There has been much discussion regarding the poor documentation that Micronesian art and material culture has received. Although the German expedition in the early 1900s collected a seemingly comprehensive selection of Micronesian material culture, they tended to focus on practical items of everyday use. While these carvings may seem to represent an insignificant episode in the craft production of Caroline Islanders in Saipan, they take on a broader significance when we see how various historic influences have blended to produce and then obliterate this figural style. The development and coalescence of this chip-carved style of statue dropped from the historical horizon a mere fifty years ago, leaving barely any record of its existence, despite the presence of photography and numerous literate researchers. This tradition was probably not only the product of several cultural influences but also the product of several different carvers, who varied in their skill and experience. These genre carvings represent the material fruit of a point in history, and their stylistic features must be evaluated in that context.

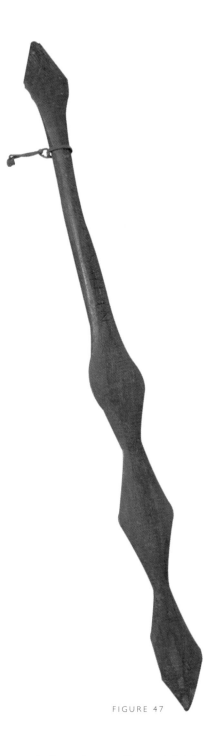

FIGURE 47

Certain Polynesian statues such as the Rapa Nui (Easter Island) *moai*, while originally having religious significance on their island of origin, have become interpreted in popular culture as "*tiki*" and have been depicted in ceramic mugs, carved lamps, and a myriad other products. The Caroline Islands squatting figure often called a "monkeyman" by outsiders has approached this level of popularity in Micronesia. It has been included in carved letter openers or used as support figures in tables; however, mostly, it has been revered as a highly variable compelling category of statuary.

During the twentieth century, unique styles of squatting figures could be found on a number of islands including Palau, Tobi,[13] Sonsorol, Yap, Ulithi, Ngulu, Lamotrek, Woleai, Satawal, and Satawan (in the Mortlocks). Most squatting figures collected range from, in rare cases, over two feet to less than two inches in height and have inlaid eyes of mother-of-pearl. Eye shape varies from a rounded, almond, or teardrop shape to triangular. Body shape varies from smooth to blocky. While squatting figures from Tobi were said by some to be used in canoe burials and as guardian figures to protect the dead, squatting figures from Ngulu (and related figures from Lamotrek and Ulithi) can be also considered symbolic of fertility, with their large bellies and swollen breasts. Figures 48 and 57 illustrates a typical Ulithi style figure, which is generally more angular and is likely to have unusually large triangular eyes. Ngulu figures, sometimes called "frogmen," also have triangular eyes but are less blocky and more fecund in appearance. They can often be distinguished by dark, painted eyebrows. Their appearance of fertility is likely related to not just human fecundity but also to the success of the breadfruit harvest. Some carvers have developed their own distinctive styles of figures and the island of origin of a statue, and sometimes even the individual carver, can be identified by evaluating its stylistic features.

Historically, islands where the Micronesian squatting figure has been collected are also known for the use of spirit canoes and the veneration of ancestral shrines. The inhabitants of Pulo Anna, Tobi, and Sonsorol

FIGURE 48

(all islands that are part of the Republic of Palau but are more closely related to Yap and Chuuk in culture) believed that the realm of the dead was a great canoe to which their souls transferred (Eilers 1936:248).[14] In Tobian canoe burials, the addition of squatting figures to the coffin may have been meant to ensure successful passage of the spirit to the afterlife. Used as household ancestor figures, the squatting statues may have also represented deceased relatives who could be propitiated to intervene on one's behalf. A personal informant, a Palauan woman whose father had a great deal of association with Tobians, was told that squatting figures were used in canoe magic. In this magical context, the squatting figure was perhaps used to absorb threatening spirits or lure them away when the model canoe in which they were placed was set adrift. This use of the canoe parallels the practice of attracting a god or beneficent spirit to the sacred canoe, which hung in the canoe house (Feldman and Rubinstein, 1986:25, 28–29). Canoes were a way to travel, so, logically, they would also be the means of support for gods and spirits. Girschner makes an interesting reference to a related practice in the Mortlock Islands where a carved image seated in a large canoe, representing an influential ancestor, is propitiated, asking the statue's permission to use the canoe and renewing it in times of war (Girschner 1911:192). Interestingly, squatting figures have been collected in the Mortlocks, such as the one from the Smithsonian Institute collection and illustrated in Kaeppler's *Oceanic Art* (Kaeppler et al. 1997:435) and another statue recently purchased by the Metropolitan Museum of Art. Figure 49 illustrates a similar carving. Such Mortlock figures often have distinctive eyebrows, which clearly echo those of the *tapuanu* masks.

However, a historical chronology of the scant literature pertaining to Caroline Island squatting figures must focus on Tobi Island, since the most popular incarnation of the motif is thought to have originated there.[15] Spanish documents make brief references to the existence of crudely carved figural sculptures in the western Carolines. However, these descriptions lack detail, and no examples of squatting figures are known to have been collected from this period. Horace Holden, an

FIGURE 49

49

FIGURE 50

American who was shipwrecked on Tobi in 1835, appears to be the earliest western contact recorded in any detail. Although he witnessed canoe burials, he does not mention squatting figures. He states, "Rudely carved figures are placed in different parts of the building and are supposed to personate their deity" (Holden 1836:43–46). The German South Sea Expedition undertaken by Krämer in the early part of the twentieth century collected a vast archive of ethnographic material throughout Micronesia. However, they only collected one anomalous example of a squatting figure in Palau. This fact can be readily understood, however, after reading Rainer Buschmann's article entitled "Tobi Captured: Converging Ethnographic and Colonial Visions on a Caroline Island." In it, Buschmann describes the social and political circumstances surrounding the expedition's one-week collecting trip to Tobi—one of the primary production areas for squatting figures. Political dissension between the chiefly and priestly groups on Tobi left the islanders suspicious of the Germans, and religious objects and practices were closely guarded during their visit (Buschmann 1996:326–327).

Anneliese Eilers, who documented the 1909 German expedition to Tobi, does not refer to squatting figures, but she does describe a sacred canoe house, which held a cult boat hung with votive offerings that had standing figures arranged at intervals (Eilers 1936:106–108). Throughout the Caroline Islands, miniature canoes were hung in canoe houses as a means of conveying the spirits of the gods. In Palau, a special boat was carved to bring a god or *chelid* to protect the community from disease. The Tobi cult boat described by Eilers was used to bring the deity into the canoe house to converse with the priest. Spirit canoes were also prominent throughout Yap and Chuuk where squatting figures were produced (Feldman and Rubinstein 1986:25, 28–29). However, figures the Germans saw being produced for trade on Tobi were described and photographed as standing, not squatting, figures. Fritz, the magistrate of Saipan, visited Tobi on the vessel *Seestern*, December 17, 1906, and provided the following description of the carvings, which Tobians were offering for trade. "They also brought remarkable pieces of carving streaked with white paint for exchange. These carvings consisted of men with hats and pipes, a complete steamship with compass, rudder, signal pipes and other details…unfinished work…however based on good observation" (Eilers 1936:31). Excellent carvers, Tobians seemed to be more comfortable making carvings that depicted foreigners and foreign objects in order to avoid a focus by outsiders on their own sacred practices.

Interestingly, Eilers describes the Tobians as "extremely conservative with regard to their traditional customs and implements and, on religious grounds, they disapprove of all innovation. Everything that comes from abroad bears, in their opinion, the seeds of misfortune. Significant is their fear of anthropological, photographic, and phonographic recordings" (Eilers 1936:92). This attitude was at least partly derived from the association between the visits of foreigners and the outbreak of disease, coupled with the repressive effects of earlier contacts with missionaries. In fact, a respiratory disease shortly following the Krämer expedition's visit killed no fewer than two hundred Tobians (Buschmann 1996:333). These considerations would certainly motivate Tobians to conceal items associated with their most sacred beliefs. However, it is also clear that Tobians shared the Yapese belief, described by Montvel-Cohen, that traditionally constructed objects contain a spirit that must be appeased by adhering to strict rituals and guidelines in the production process. As Holden points out, the Tobians were afraid that their god Yarris would become angry unless the metal fishhooks they were given were reshaped into the traditional shape used in their tortoiseshell hooks (Holden 1836:43). Eager to obtain trade goods, the Tobians worked hard to create objects they thought would interest westerners; however, they were very reticent in allowing visitors to see or handle ritual objects. It was with great difficulty that Krämer's wife, Elizabeth, obtained permission to sketch their sacred boat.

Dr. Donald Rubinstein, professor of anthropology and public health at the University of Guam, was told by an elderly female informant that, in her youth, during the first decade of the twentieth century, she remem

人形の側面

FIGURE 51

51

bered seeing a spirit house on Tobi, which held a figure two feet tall resembling a modern "monkeyman" (*Nature's Way* 2005). This recollection provides more anecdotal evidence to support the idea that Tobian religious practices may not have been fully documented during German times. Fortunately, Japanese researchers, such as Kenji Kiyono and Atsushi Someki, were able to collect anecdotal information on the traditional use of figural sculpture on Tobi before pre-contact religious practices were completely abandoned in favor of Christianity.

The Japanese who took over the administration of Micronesia in 1919 had a better understanding of Micronesian spiritual beliefs. While they allowed some European Christian missionaries to continue their activities, Japan's own religion, the practice of Shinto, included the veneration of ancestral shrines, as did Micronesian traditional religion. Atsushi Someki was a Japanese artist and ethnologist who visited Micronesia in 1931. He described the Tobi *ninyo* or Tobi "dolls" he encountered as ancestor figures, which the Tobians kept in special places and in their homes. Someki felt that the artistic merit of the Tobian figures was limited. He preferred standing *mog mog* figures from Chuuk and probably related figures from Woleai and Ulithi. Someki found only one carver on Tobi in 1934, Oakama, who could still carve fine examples of the traditional Tobi doll. The Tobian chief Mokonukuro could also carve them but not as skillfully. Tobi dolls carved in Palau could still be obtained, but they were expensive, and Someki felt that even those carved by Tobians who had moved to Palau were no longer truly authentic (Someki 1945:304–307).

Kenji Kiyono was a Japanese ethnologist who visited Palau in 1941. He sought to understand the cultural origins of the Japanese people by studying Micronesian cultures. Although he discovered that squatting figures, said to have originated on Tobi, could be purchased in Palau, like Someki, he considered these little better than copies. According to him, only one traditional carver was still left, probably Oakama. However, Tobi informants related that once, long ago, Tobi Islanders carved big

FIGURE 52

and small statues. Near the big figures, they placed the smaller figures, which they prayed to and worshiped like gods. Kiyono further related that Spanish missionaries had succeeded in suppressing the production of the large figures, but the small figures continued to be produced. According to the Tobians, the original figures were carved in soft woods, while later copies began to be produced in hardwoods. This change may have simply been a function of the availability of better tools for wood-working following European contact. The original figures were found in pairs, identified as male and female by their different parts. Genuine Tobi dolls were also identified by their eyes, which tended to point upwards on the tops of sloping foreheads (Figures 50 and 51). Tobians used their canoes for coffins, cutting them and sealing them up after first placing a pair of Tobi figures inside (generally one male and one female) to function as guardians to accompany the dead.

FIGURE 53

One squatting figure, collected by Yoshio Kondo, conchologist with the Bishop Museum expedition to Micronesia in 1936, is now in the Bishop Museum in Honolulu. The figure is accompanied by a catalog note reading, "Said to be buried with chiefs in lieu of humans." However, Kiyono admits that the details of these practices have been obscured, due to the influence of Spanish missionaries. Interestingly, Kiyono adds that the Palauans traditionally had a similar figure, which could be differentiated from the Tobian figure by the fact that it had tattoo marks. Additionally, the female mons on the Palauan "doll" was represented by a triangle pointing downwards, similar to those seen on the *dilukai* figure traditionally hung over the entrance to the Palauan *bai*. Tobi figures, however, generally have the mons pointing upwards represented by a sort of "w" shape whereby the clitoris is outlined in the center at its upwards point (Kiyono 1942:679–681).

Tobian figures may have originally been more angular in form, similar to Ngulu and Ulithi squatting figures. The smooth sculptural style currently associated with the Tobi style figure may have evolved in response to Japanese aesthetic standards. In any case, a period of popularity and high

FIGURE 54

FIGURE 55

production for the squatting figures began during the Japanese period and ultimately resulted in a proliferation of styles associated with specific carvers. The Japanese liked these squatting figures and trained Palauan carvers to make them in the same classes in which they taught them to carve storyboards. Four statues in a style illustrated in Someki's book have an almost sumo-like stance (Figure 54).

Micronesian sculpture continued to be created during the American period; however, by then, the original cultural significance and appearance of these figures had become obscure. After WWII, during the first years of the Trust Territory, Micronesia was generally a restricted military area, and there was little tourism. Although the government bought crafts to encourage the island economies, they advised carvers to spend more time on the carvings they had already started, since only a limited quantity of handicrafts could be purchased. When Dr. Eugenie Clark, a research ichthyologist, visited Ngulu as part of a research initiative funded by the U.S. Navy shortly after WWII, she stated, "Unlike most of the other islands, Ngulu did not sell copra. Its major products were sculptured wooden figures which the Island Trading Company called 'frogmen.' Actually, they were heavy-browed, triangular-faced, pregnant women symbolizing fertility. Several hundred figures ranging from a few inches to nearly two feet were lined up on the beach. Some were carefully carved; others were chipped out hastily to meet the new large demand of the ITC [Island Trading Company], which was selling them in Koror like hotcakes. Lt. [Harry] Stille [a member of U.S. Navy personnel who bought crafts for the Trust Territory gift shops] wisely bought only the well-carved figures" (Clark 1953:157–158). The selection of better quality sculptures for purchase may have had the effect of improving the quality of the carvings, but the number of squatting figures produced declined. Nowadays, a few such figures are carved in styles distinctive to the artist. For example, squatting figures, carved by Patricio Tahimaremamo during the 1960s (Figure 56), sometimes have distinctive batman ears. Examples can still be found, in a variety of styles and some especially interesting examples were collected immediately after WWII. However, few pre-twentieth-century examples of this style of figure have been identified, even in German museums. One squatting figure with inlaid eyes and an enormous phallus was collected on Palau by the Krämer expedition and is now in the Linden Museum in Germany. Though this figure exhibits some stylistic similarities to later squatting figures, it also has several distinctive features, including a hat, and elaborate pierced ears with carved-on earrings. This carving may have represented one of the figures that were sometimes placed on either side of the feet of the *dilukai* figure on the front of the Palauan *bai*, a statuary tradition unlikely to be related to the Tobian squatting figure.

Certainly, the squatting figure motif cannot have originated solely on Tobi. It is seen in figures ranging as far away as Polynesia, Indonesia, New Guinea, and the Solomons. All of these groups have similarities in art and material culture, which are very likely the result of pre-western contact and exchange. It makes sense that the squatting figure motif is a worldwide phenomenon, since squatting and sitting on the floor are natural positions in indigenous cultures where western-styled chairs are not customarily used. In fact, sitting is considered the traditional posture of authority on Yap, so gods or ancestor images could logically be portrayed in a sitting posture (Montvel-Cohen 1982:95). This motif represents the perfect ancestral archetype, since the squatting position simultaneously symbolizes birth and death. In western Micronesian nations, as in many other cultures, the traditional burial position is with knees drawn upward against the chest, while the act of childbirth often involves a similar position. Thus, the circular and continuous nature of life is personified and reaffirmed.

During the German, Japanese, and American periods, more and more Tobians were transferred to Palau and other islands following storms and storm-related famines. In the second half of the twentieth century, a generation of Tobians grew up exposed to urbanization and Christianity and became increasingly willing to purvey images once sacred to their traditional culture into popular *tiki* icons. Latecomers to the administration

FIGURE 56

55

FIGURE 57

of Micronesia, the Americans were left to question whether the squatting figure ever really had ritual significance. However, in 1968, a crude, blocky, stone carving of an anatomically correct squatting figure was uncovered on Tobi by anthropologist Peter Black.[16] Informants stated that this carving was one of a series of figures once placed around the house of the "mother of the island" where children too young for canoe burials were interred. Ultimately, it appeared that Europeans had removed the other stone figures in the series, probably in an attempt to suppress traditional religious practices (Black 1979:349–353). But, while there were brief visits from missionaries beginning much earlier, the Catholic Church, the first church to become established in this island group, was not formally ensconced until quite late in the colonial process—1928 for Ulithi and 1931 for Tobi (Hezel 1991:20, 218). Japanese accounts, collected while knowledgeable informants were still available, provide a crucial window into the early belief systems of Micronesians, as well as an early description of carving styles. Many Japanese accounts have not yet been translated, and there are, hopefully, more descriptions and documents still to be discovered. Meanwhile, this once-sacred souvenir continues to intrigue us with echoes from an earlier time.

FIGURE 58

CHAPTER TWO

Storyboards
to Graphics THE EVOLUTION OF MICRONESIAN ILLUSTRATION

The Republic of Palau (Belau) is known throughout the Pacific for its skillful and highly creative storyboards, which, today, are made into many shapes and sizes, and are sometimes even incorporated into furniture. Palauan storyboards are derived from the decorated gable beams and interior crossbeams that originally ornamented Palauan clubhouses or *bai*. The traditional *bai* was a public building that served as a focus for village activities such as dances or feasts as well as providing a lodging place for visiting men. It was a center for the men's social life and provided a place for the chief's council meetings. Women were only rarely allowed the use of the *bai* during designated time periods but sometimes, in very wealthy villages, could have their own *bai*. Palauans also built shrines, which generally housed the gods associated with a specific clan and were located near the clan chief's meeting house. There were also special decorated buildings for powerful holy men or inspired priests (Jernigan 1973:32–39). Canoe houses were also decorated and acted as a meeting place for fishermen and a place to store canoes. They were usually located at the boat landing. Today many modern buildings in Palau are decorated with motifs derived from the *bai*. There has also been a revival in the building of traditional *bai*. Visitors can see several examples of this impressive type of building, constructed without nails, screws, or pegs of any kind, including the one on the grounds of the Belau National Museum in Koror.

Building a *bai* was an important part of competition and status seeking in Palauan society. In order to build one under the most prestigious

FIGURE 59

circumstances, it was necessary to hire an expert builder from another village. The *bai* was built and decorated in pieces and then erected on the spot. Ritual payments and feasting were involved in the construction process, so only wealthy clans could finance such an event. The only carved boards produced independently of *bai* at this time were used as templates to record customary stories. Otherwise, storyboards were only seen in the rafters and on the gable front as part of the traditional structure (Jernigan 1973:122–130). In fact, some people believe that the Palauan *bai* only began to be extensively decorated when the English Captain Henry Wilson provided Palauans with metal tools after his shipwreck in 1783. However, as Jernigan points out, when the HMS *Panther* and HMS *Endeavor* returned to Palau five years later, as a follow up to Wilson's well-documented shipwreck, the Reverend John P. Hockin described the *bai* as having an inside that was "curiously worked and ornamented with various flowers and figures. The ends have much appearances of Gendoo temples" (Hockin 1803). Jernigan concludes that it is unlikely that Palauan architectural style should have changed so dramatically in a mere five years (Jernigan 1973:23). Therefore, while Palauan architectural decoration may have flourished after the introduction of metal tools, it is likely that this cultural tradition was much older.

Early decorations on the *bai* were customarily painted in four naturally obtained pigments—black, white, red, and yellow. Also, most story-boards generally portrayed small, wavy lines issuing from the mouths of figures to depict speech. These are known as "speech scrolls." The boards were used to relate historic incidents, promote traditional values, and preserve traditional myths and stories, while sometimes humorously shaming other villages. Standard categories included stories of heroes, tricksters, gods, and creation myths. For example, the story of Tebang tells of a young man who went to live with his new wife's family. Since Tebang's mother had died years before, his father lived with him. But, one day, Tebang grew tired of his father and simply asked him to leave. His father returned to his birth village and found that his relatives were gone and, thus, he no longer had a house in which to live. Tebang's father

FIGURE 60

was, by this time, old and weak. Because he could not fish for himself, he had to rely on handouts from other villagers. Without a home of his own, he had to live in the village *bai*. Tebang, however, had forgotten about his father because he was so busy with the activities of his wife's village. One day, Tebang cut down a huge tree and began to hollow it out to form a canoe. When he tried to push it down the bank to the water, immediately, without the proper observances to the tree spirits, it became stuck in a taro patch. Tebang and all his fellow villagers tried vigilantly but could not free the stuck canoe. Finally, they went to consult a diviner who told him that the tree spirits were angry. He advised Tebang to seek the wisdom of his father for a solution about how to appease the tree spirits. Tebang went to his home village and brought his father, who was weak with malnutrition, back with him. His father was able to recall a rhythmic chant that appeased the tree spirits and enabled all the young men to pull together and free the canoe. This story is an example of one that promotes traditional values, in this case the importance of showing proper respect to the gods and to one's parents. Versions of this story and others can be found in Jerome Esebei Temengil's *Legends of Old Palau* (Temengil 2004:52).

During the German period, the Germans collected a great deal of information about the decorations on clubhouses. Much of it was recorded by the Krämer expedition in the early 1900s. Most of the structures they documented have now been destroyed by tropical storms and have not been rebuilt. To many outsiders, the *bai* was seen as a place for "immoral" activities and a way to perpetuate the native religion, so the building of these structures was eventually prohibited by the German government. A drop in population from disease also meant that labor was not available to maintain old structures. Later, bombing during WWII destroyed even more *bai*; however, today, there has been a revival, and new *bai* have been built (Kitalong 1998:144–145).

FIGURE 61

FIGURE 62

After WWI, Palau became an administrative center for the Japanese colonial empire in Micronesia. It became a popular destination for Japanese tourists and colonists. The Japanese were generally accepting of traditional Palauan culture. They began to encourage the Palauans to carve small boards as souvenirs, but they expected them to be in traditional colors and to retain the stylistic primitivism of the original *bai* boards, including an incised border depicting traditional symbolic motifs. The Japanese scholar Hijikata Hisakatsu became involved in training Palauans to carve small boards as souvenirs in 1929 (Figure 62). He selected young men with talent and taught them the basic principles of art, as well as the details of a limited number of traditional stories previously recorded by the Germans. Ngiraibuuch, Osiik, and Sbal were among the storyboard artists he trained. The fact that these artists worked with a limited number of stories (approximately thirty-three) continues to have an effect on storyboards to the present (Jernigan 1973:150). Due to the limited selection of stories, the more popular stories may be produced again and again in slightly different styles. By repeatedly refining and developing a single theme, the artist is able to devote more attention to the structure of the composition. These changes in structure can be understood by comparing earlier and later versions of the same story. Further, the stories were not always depicted on the boards directionally, from left to right, to show a sequence of scenes in order, as we would see in a comic strip graphic. While some stories showed the action from left to right, others were right to left (in the

Japanese literary tradition). Still other boards showed the key scene in the center and related scenes on either side. The storyboard artists also generally produced more than one identical storyboard. Uniqueness was not a condition for the production of this genre of art.

During the early American period immediately after WWII, few storyboards were signed and they were all carved in a very similar style which Jernigan refers to as "new style" (Figure 69). These boards were often very long—five feet or more. They usually had a zigzag border, and the story was incised into a natural, wooden background, unlike the painted-white backgrounds of the early style rafter boards. Artists also began to use commercial pigments, adding blues, greens, and browns to the traditional palette of black, white, red, and yellow with which figures, trees, and *bai* were customarily painted. The figures, especially male ones, shown on the board were generally depicted in frenetic activity. According to Jernigan, new style boards were relatively uniform in style. However, some individual differences between artists can readily be identified, most notably the size and coloration of the figures and other features in relation to the height of the board. Artists creating early new style boards left more blank space, while later storyboard artists tended to fill up the board so little empty space was left. Finally, there was a change in borders from the traditional "row of triangles" or *kldarem* border to the new *kliuch* or tridacna clam border (Jernigan 1973:158–162). This style of border can be seen on Figure 3.

FIGURE 63

FIGURE 64

FIGURE 65

A departure from this "new style" occurred early in the American administration of Micronesia. Faced with a limited market for sales, some Palauan artists began to produce "luxury boards," which U.S. administrators in Guam or other areas of the Trust Territory could hang in their offices (Jernigan 1973:181). These boards, some painted and many unpainted, were large and richly detailed and, in the 1950s and 1960s, were quite expensive, some priced at over one-hundred dollars. The price of storyboards was generally calculated per square inch.

There also began to be a distinction between pornographic and non-pornographic storyboards. Originally, some illustrations on the *bai* had involved graphic depictions of enlarged sex organs. However, Palauans began to realize that, while these subjects might titillate some servicemen, many Americans did not find these subjects acceptable. They began to show figures wearing clothing, when traditionally they had been naked. As storyboards continued to develop during the American period, individual storyboard artists began to sign their work more often and began to develop unique and identifiable styles. A variety of borders were used, and backgrounds were excised on the painted storyboards. Figures and objects were arranged on the boards to decorate more of the field while expressing the story in a more concise manner.

Unpainted boards carved in relief using native hardwoods such as *dort* or *ifil* became popular with Americans in the 1960s and 1970s. These board exists as the most commonly produced style to this day. They were often deeply carved and sometimes dyed with shoe polish or inlaid with mother-of-pearl. A style of carving unpainted storyboards (Figure 67), generally known as "prison style," is often adopted by inmates who use their carving skills to earn money while incarcerated. The development of this style is generally attributed to a storyboard artist known as Baris Sylvester. In the "prison style," figures are generally shown to a more European standard of more full-bodied women with flowing hair, as opposed to the traditional hairstyle, which is knotted into a bun.

The famous carver Osiik was also known for deeply carved, unpainted boards and developed a unique style of producing abstract, energetic figures along with distinctive caterpillar-like speech scrolls, which have been compared to the work of Matisse (Kagle 1976:15) (Figure 63). An extremely productive storyboard artist called Ngiraibuuch produced many highly painted boards (Figure 3). He continued to produce a modified version of the traditional painted board long after many other carvers had begun to focus on unpainted boards. Today, his son Linus Ngiraibuuch continues to produce painted boards that are often based on early storyboard designs recorded during German times.

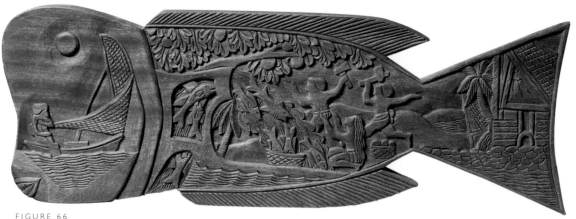

FIGURE 66

FIGURE 67

During the early post-WWII period, storyboard artists produced "new style" boards, which continued to portray the *bai* or men's house as it had been traditionally depicted—from a one-dimensional side view. Then, in the late 1950s and early 1960s, when luxury boards began to be carved, painted boards started to depict the bai with depth perspective. The building now appeared to recede into the board, while the painted gable face was partly obscured by the overhang of the roof. This switch to depth perspective in the depiction of the *bai* was introduced by Bernardino Rdulaol (Figure 67), who studied modern painting techniques with visiting artists during the Japanese period (Jernigan 1973:209–210). Although the Japanese discouraged innovation, Rdulaol was able to sell trays with the *bai* shown in perspective. Later, during the American period, "'the perspective *bai*' came to be the exclusive kind of *bai* representation probably because it has greater visual interest" (Jernigan 1973:170). With the exception of Rdulaol, however, depth perspective in figures continued to be shown only through the overlapping of limbs, typically of legs not arms. This change in the depiction of the *bai* provides an excellent guideline for dating the age of a board. During the late 1950s, storyboard artists began to include the perspective *bai* in unpainted boards, which were just becoming popular. The perspective *bai* is still used in unpainted boards today.

Today, some boards are organized vertically instead of horizontally, while others are shaped like fish, crocodiles, or turtles. Some boards are mass-produced, and workmanship can be rough. Artists often focus on the one key scene or action, which clearly defines the story. Many boards are produced by prisoners in the Koror Jail workshop. In recent years, the Breadfruit Tree Story and the Egg Laying Cycle of the Turtle Story were some of the most popular stories depicted. Custom-made items like coffee tables or skillfully carved elaborate boards are being made in specialized workshops. The Tebang Wood Carving Shop, for example, uses a blend of Osiik's figural style and Rdulaol's use of pigment to create a sophisticated distinctive product. Ling Inabo, the master carver who owns the Tebang studio, is known for producing very large commissions

FIGURE 68

FIGURE 69

for hotels and banks on Palau and elsewhere. Zacharius Omengebar was another talented carver, who passed away in 2006. He created distinctive boards for many years. Richard Silmai, a free thinker, produces storyboards (Figure 69) based on Krämer's early 1900s sketches of *bai*, as well as modern boards with satirical political messages. His workshop is located in the local gym in Koror where many of his boards are on display.

The quality of carving can be impressive, and storyboards can be expensive, running from seventy-five to several hundred dollars, depending on the artist and the size of the board. Storyboard coffee tables may cost from several hundred to over a thousand dollars. The medium has become so popular that storyboards are also now being produced on islands like Yap and Chuuk.

GRAPHIC ARTS IN PALAU AND YAP

The artistic tradition of the storyboard was expanded in 1970's Palau to include the graphic arts, specifically watercolor. Charles Gibbons is one storyboard artist who later became a famous folk artist and has had his work depicted on several Palauan stamps. Born in 1888, he acted as an interpreter, informant, and judge and was honored by the chiefly title of *Rechucher* in 1943. Conferred by the men's council, *Rechucher* is a Palauan word meaning "messenger," and the title carried the responsibility for military operations in olden days (Owen 1980:6). Gibbons was over seventy when he began to draw detailed scenes of traditional Palauan life. He was educated during the German period and later worked for both the German and Japanese administrations as interpreter, and, later, constable. Gibbons's West Indian grandfather had taught his family English, so Gibbons was well prepared to become an interpreter for the Americans after WWII. He began working as a resident informant and artist at the Belau National Museum in 1959. Gibbons was famous for his large, extremely detailed watercolors depicting Palauan life in a time when fishing, warfare, and feasting were relatively unaffected by western influence. He held several exhibits of his art with the assistance of founding member of the Belau National Museum Hera Ware Owen, including

FIGURE 70

one in Seattle (1971), one in Guam (1973), and one in Saipan (1980). He passed away in 1988. He is best known for detailed, miniature, cultural scenes in watercolor, although often on a much grander scale than is shown in Figure 71, where men are depicted performing a war dance before a *bai*. Gibbons lived through many exciting times in Palauan history before embarking on his late-life watercolorist career.

FIGURE 71

Artist Ruth Glenn Little visited Yap several times during the early 1990s. In 1994, she moved there, staying for several years, during which time she taught young, talented Yapese artists how to paint. Students participated in a project to make alphabet cards for local schools and to illustrate books. As a result of her efforts, watercolor has become a very lively artistic tradition in Yap where artists, including Tommy Tamangmed (Figure 72) from the village of Gargey on Yap and Luke Holoi from Lothow Island in the Ulithi group, produce beautiful watercolors of cultural scenes such as the performance of dances, outriggers at sea, and underwater sea life. Traditional tattoos, grass skirts, stone money, and other aspects of Yapese and outer-island life are portrayed in loving detail.

Palauan storyboard carvers as well as contemporary Yapese and Palauan graphic artists each find their own unique ways to reinforce and perpetuate elements of their traditional cultures while providing an outlet for individual creative expression. Now that brushes, paint, and a variety of other art materials are available, and art is being taught in schools throughout Micronesia, watercolors, acrylics, and other media have increasingly become significant modes of expression.

FIGURE 72

CHAPTER THREE

Tools and Trade
in Island Life

On remote islands such as those of Micronesia, materials used to make containers are dependent on available resources. Not every island has clay appropriate for making pottery, for example. On low islands, such as those in the Marshalls or Kiribati, appropriate wood to carve bowls is in short supply. On the other hand, coconuts are nearly always available, and skillfully constructed baskets can usefully function as containers in many contexts.

Pottery making is an ancient tradition in western Micronesia, where it has been found in archaeological sites on a number of islands including the Marianas, Palau, and Yap. Samples from Saipan have been found to date as early as 1100 to 1500 B.C. (Butler 1995:33). When artist and scholar Hijikata Hisakatsu traveled to Palau in 1929, he observed that people were still familiar with traditional paddle and anvil pottery-making techniques using coils of clay, which are then smoothed together and fired on a simple open hearth (Osborne 1966:31–39). However, from the number of decorated pot shards that Hijikata observed, he concluded that this pottery-making tradition was once much more prevalent (Hijikata 1991:20–21). A general decline in the production of pottery due to a shortage of appropriate clay may have begun prior to western contact. However, the advent of Europeans, and later Japanese, with their metal cook pots and sophisticated glazed ceramics, must have further eroded the pro-

FIGURE 73

FIGURE 74

71

FIGURE 75

duction of traditional paddle and anvil pottery, as a dependence on the newly available containers grew. Certainly, by the American period, very few Palauans were practicing pottery making, though some traditional lamps decorated with Palauan figures were being made for trade.

Although leaves were often used for serving or to wrap foods for cooking, several types of vessels, including gourds, coconuts, and carved bowls, were in common use at the time of western contact. Carved bowls took a variety of forms. In Palau, the *ongal* was a flat platter with fishtail-shaped handles used to serve fish at feasts. Another traditional Palauan product was a small, lidded container often inlaid with mother-of-pearl and used to store coconut candy or valuables such as bead money. Long, low tables with many legs, also inlaid with mother-of-pearl, were used to present taro at feasts. While Palauans are known for their fish platters, flat round bowls, taro tables, and covered containers (Figure 75), all inlaid with mother-of-pearl, Yapese are known for their hanging, bird-shaped bowls used to store pigments for painting (Figure 76), as well as their oblong tackle boxes, also produced on the islands between Yap and Chuuk. The tackle box is a tightly lidded, wooden box that has been pierced with holes so that a cord could assist in keeping the lid affixed.

FIGURE 76

72

It was carved in several distinctive forms (Figure 74). This box was used to keep betel nut and other personal items dry on long ocean voyages (Steager 1979:346). Kapingamarangi Atoll is known for its distinctive oval bowls in a variety of sizes with handles on one end and matching notched pounders. Chuuk has deeply carved breadfruit bowls with fishtailed handles. Kubary has said, regarding Chuukese bowls, "The manufacture of wooden receptacles occupy the prominent place in the [Chuuk] wood industry, and this is all the more surprising since [they] do not take their food from wooden dishes but…[use large leaves as dishes]…. Wooden receptacles used for preparing turmeric, as well as for exposing food provided on festive occasions, take the place of money and are employed particularly in relationships between the clans, at peace conferences and other settlements" (Kubary 1889:54).

Another interesting form of container is called an *omail* in Palau, but it is found in nearly every island group. It consists of an open coconut shell (Figure 77). The rim is pierced, and it is suspended using handmade twine. During the Ninth Festival of Pacific Arts, which was held in Palau in 2004, several examples of *omail* were collected by the author from different areas of Palau, including Angaur, Melekeok and Sonsorol (Sonsoral), as well as from the island of Yap. Some styles have a lid attached, and some are hung from three strings, while others are hung from only two. These containers are used for carrying water and collecting palm sap for making *tuba* or coconut wine. The winemaker must climb up the palm tree and cut into the coconut flower, collecting the sap in the coconut bowl where it rapidly ferments (within a day or so). Each distinct island people developed unique and recognizable variations for this basic storage object. In Kiribati, for example, the coconut is encased in a kind of sling of knotted rope.

Some carved bowls are valued heirlooms and may be used for feasts and special celebrations. However, the availability of western-styled containers has greatly reduced the production and use of traditional carved bowls. Today, relatively few are made, some just for the tourist trade.

FIGURE 77

73

Before western contact, the primary way to travel the long distances between islands was by outrigger canoe. Two basic types of outrigger canoe were used. Paddling canoes had no sail and were used to fish within a protected lagoon. They were generally smaller and more maneuverable. Sailing canoes were used to take longer trips between islands and sometimes for warfare. The largest were used on the open ocean, while smaller canoes were used inside lagoons or barrier reefs. Model canoes were traditionally made on many islands as racing toys for children, to practice canoe-making skills on a smaller scale, and, on some islands, to be used in traditional magic. In Chuuk, breadfruit and fish were traditionally "called" through rituals of sustenance, which included the construction of a special model canoe. The canoe had crescent moon prows similar to those of the hanging double canoes seen by Krämer, which were used to call the gods into the canoe house. The fish or breadfruit "summoner" was a specialized practitioner whose sacred knowledge or *roong* was passed along as property in specific lineages. Ritual observances, including taboos on certain foods and the making of medicinal offerings to specially selected breadfruit trees, were highlighted by a canoe race in which the summoner's model canoe was raced against other canoes. Generally, the summoner's canoe was allowed to win so that the harvest could be plentiful (Goodenough 2002:199–204). Breadfruit and fish are both associated with canoes, since canoes, constructed from breadfruit wood, are used to catch fish. Canoes, then, were not only toys later replicated for the tourist trade but also important objects that every man needed to know how to construct to ensure the community's ample food supply. Each island group in Micronesia has at least one unique, traditional style and sometimes several different styles of canoe for different purposes. On Kapingamarangi Atoll, for example, the traditional sailing canoe is no longer recalled (Haddon and Hornell 1991:397–398), but beautiful outrigger models of paddling canoes are produced with sails included, which may have been adapted from the traditional Pohnpei sailing canoe. The Marshall Islands are known for their detailed model racing canoes called *korkor*, while Yapese *powpow* canoes, traditionally painted red, black, and white, are readily identifiable

FIGURE 78

by their characteristic v-shaped prows. The black and yellow outrigger (Figure 79) was collected by Ted Bayer, who was part of the Marston Bates expedition to Ifaluk (Ifalik) that is described in *Coral Island: Portrait of an Atoll*. The canoe is labeled as having been purchased October 28, 1953, a time when Bayer was actively participating in the expedition. It is uncertain on which island this canoe was collected; however, museum administrator Mandy Etpison advised that black and yellow are canoe colors used only on Satawal.

Apart from canoes, other ocean-related items include wooden, carved canoe bailers, canoe paddles, tackle boxes, stick navigation charts, and fishing equipment, including nets, hooks, and sinks. Fish traps of various kinds are another item of cultural and artistic interest. The fish trap shown here (Figure 80) is a model; however, when full size, it takes four men to position. It is placed in an area where the tide drains water through a narrows so that fish are funneled inside the trap and then not able to find their way out. Traditional bailers were usually cut from breadfruit wood and had carved handles attached. Bailers today are generally carved for the tourist trade and from somewhat harder woods. Montvel-Cohen has observed that, on Woleai, chlorine bleach containers cut diagonally have largely replaced traditional wooden canoe bailers (Montvel-Cohen 1987:8). This is good example of recycling using found objects in the context of scarce resources on remote islands.

Stick navigation charts are a fascinating representation of geographic knowledge extending far beyond immediate surroundings in that they demonstrate the indigenous knowledge of wind and wave patterns around and between islands. Originating in the Marshall Islands, the stick chart is a series of sticks tied together, sometimes with shells added to mark the location of islands or sandbars. The angles of the sticks in relation to the shells illustrate the patterns of waves as they respond to the presence of atolls and reefs. Stick charts act as maps to aid in navigation as well as teach novices the patterns of waves surrounding islands. There are several different forms of stick charts. One covers an entire

chain of islands (*rebbelib*), another is used for specific voyages and only covers a limited number of islands (*medo*), while a third is small and square-shaped and is used for teaching about currents around a specific island when traveling between two atolls (*wappepe*) (Mulford 2006:7–8).

Fishing is an essential subsistence activity for most islanders as it provides the main source of protein. A variety of throw nets and hand nets are used, including one commonly called the butterfly net, often used by women in Chuuk in cooperative fishing. Fishhooks are usually backed with mother-of-pearl and have a small tortoiseshell hook attached. The fishing sink from Palau, the Marshall Islands, and many other island groups is generally made from leopard cowries with a portion of the line stuffed into the aperture of the shell, thus attaching it. Cowry shells prepared like this are also seen as part of traditional octopus lures.

FIGURE 82

Transactions between different island groups in Micronesia often took the form of tribute, involving such commodities as betel nut, turmeric, tobacco, breadfruit, and taro. Due to variations in weather and environment, at any given time, some islands had more plentiful supplies of these crops than others. High islands had large trees, which could be used to make canoes, and, more importantly, they could act as safe refuge for atoll dwellers fleeing from the ravages of typhoons and droughts (Alkire 1989:4–6). Smaller islands tended to use specialized crafts as a valuable medium of exchange. Outer islands paid tribute to chiefs of Yap proper (the high island) using *tur* or *lava lava*. Elaborate *lava lava*, called *machi*, were especially prized (Figure 83). *Machi* were traditionally woven for the paramount chief of the tribute island who, in turn, might give it to his tribute recipient on Yap (Rubinstein 1988:62–63). These intricate ritual textiles were also used as funerary wrappings for chiefs on Yap. Regular *lava lava* also known as *tur* were used, along with foods like cooked breadfruit and taro, in kin-based exchanges such as marriages and funerals within smaller, outer-island communities like Lamotrek or Ulithi. These textiles were valuable and labor intensive and constituted a very important part of women's work.

Specialized forms of money for traditional transactions were developed on both Palau and Yap. Indeed, Yap is known throughout the world for its giant stone money (Figure 84). Sometimes taller than the height of a man, this money is the largest and, many say, the most unusual form of money in the world. It consists of stone wheels of crystallized calcite shaped like millstones that were mined in Palau, 250 miles from Yap, and originally transported across the ocean on rafts attached to outrigger canoes. Many Yapese were killed in storms and accidents during transport, and, therefore, stone money was relatively rare, as well as somewhat restricted in size. These stone wheels, called *rai*, could be as small as seven inches across but were mined in larger and larger sizes once European traders, such as O'Keefe, supplied iron tools for mining and began to transport the stone wheels on sailing ships in exchange for loads of copra (dried coconut) and *bêche de mer* (dried sea cucumber). Yap had

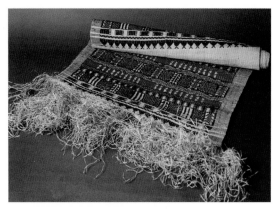

FIGURE 83

FIGURE 84

FIGURE 85

13,000 pieces of stone money by 1929 (Gilliland 1975:21), and some of those, which had been transported by the legendary Captain O'Keefe, were as wide as three-and-three-quarters yards in diameter. Unfortunately, many pieces were broken by the Japanese during WWII and used as filler in the construction of roads.

When the Germans first purchased Micronesian territories from the Spanish, they had a difficult time recruiting labor for public works projects such as the roads encircling each island. Island economies were not built on wage labor, and people used clubhouse membership, kinship, and other affiliations to gain help for community projects. Stone money was stored in "banks," which is to say in rows alongside village paths or leaning up against the sides of buildings. Whenever a financial transaction occurred using the money, its location was not changed. Everyone simply understood that the particular piece of money involved in the transaction now belonged to someone different. The newly installed German governor on Yap, Arno Senfft, thought of a way to exploit the stone money system. He worked through the chiefs to recruit labor, and, whenever German laws on Yap were breached, he painted a large "BA" for *Bezirksamt*, or District Office, on the offender's stone money. This mark indicated the German's possession of the stone money. Senfft would not permit the mark to be removed until the Yapese had provided the requested labor (Hezel 1995:105–107).

Since the western discovery of the giant stone money on Yap, it has been a popular curiosity for outsiders. In the fall of 1965, Yapese law prohibited the removal of Yapese stone money from the island without official taxation and approval of the transaction by the Yapese government (Gilliland 1975:18). This and later legislation has made it virtually impossible for genuine pieces of stone money to be removed from Yap, although occasionally museums obtain a special permit. However, copies were already being made prior to 1965, many from larger pieces of broken money. Currently, stone money that is carved for trade is usually six or seven inches in diameter. Smoothly carved pieces with smoothly pierced central holes are less likely to be genuine than the worn or chipped pieces that also show discoloration due to age. One also sees representations of Yapese stone money incorporated in bookends and sculptures, and stone money continues to be a popular theme on Yapese, as well as Palauan, storyboards.

Other forms of currency were used in lesser transactions on Yap, including the gold lip clamshell, most commonly found in Palau but also obtained from the Philippines and New Guinea. A single shell, called a *yar*, like the replica pictured in Figure 86, was presented with a woven handle attached. Variations of this form have the sides of the shell broken off, after which they are called *thiloy*, and sometimes boar's teeth are attached on each side. To break the shells, they were buried in the ground and a small fire was built around them causing the shell to break off at the sand line. Such shell currency was considered more valuable because of the extra effort involved in its creation.[17] Many pieces of large clams were attached by a network of hand-woven cords in groups of three, five, or seven, in a related form of shell money sometimes referred to as a dowry today. In yet another form of shell money, the hinge of a giant clamshell was carved into a kind of pestle shaped like a tusk (*ma*), which fitted into a wooden mortar. Several types of Yapese shell money or *yar* are still being made on Yap Island today, both for trade and actual use. Lengths of rope wound into skeins of fifty or one hundred feet also function as money. Men roll this rope, or sennit, by hand on their knees—a common activity for older men in the canoe house. Such rope was undoubtedly

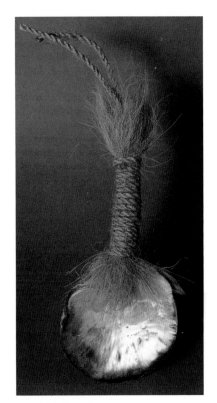

FIGURE 86

FIGURE 87

FIGURE 88

valued by early trading ships that needed replacements for their rigging. Yapese and a few other Micronesian groups, especially in the Central Carolines, make this rope. Still being made today, one hundred feet of Yapese rope cost approximately one hundred dollars in 2006.

Palauans also use several types of traditional money. The most precious are antique beads, foreign in construction, including what appear to be pieces of a type of glass bracelet or armlet that have been drilled to be used as a bead. A bracelet section is then worn as a pendant on a string. Other types of bead money can be classified by shape—prismatic, round, oval, or cylindrical. Collections of these beads are proudly worn by Palauan women and were traditionally used in important transactions, including negotiating for peace following a battle. The beads appear to be made from such materials as fired clay, green glass, and opaque polychrome glass. However, Douglas Osborne, archaeologist, who conducted an extensive survey of Palau from December 1953 through June of 1954, was convinced that the large "gorgets" contained mineral components such as jasper. It is true that one test for the authenticity of bead money is its ability to scratch regular glass. The presence of a mineral such as jasper may explain why these beads appear to be harder than regular glass and, thus, able to scratch it (Osborne 1966:477–494). Since the original pieces of bead money and bracelet sections were introduced, perhaps from the wreck of an Asian ship, no additional bead money has been introduced into the system of bead money exchange until recent times. Today, however, Palauans sometimes purchase additional antique beads, since similar beads and bracelets have been found in metal age gravesites. Paul Rainbird, department head and senior lecturer in archeology at the University of Wales, states in his book *The Archeology of Micronesia*, that similar beads have been found in graves in the Philippines dating between 800 and 400 years ago and in the islands of South East Asia approximately 2,000 years ago (Rainbird 2004:147). Women of high social rank still proudly wear their bead money on necklace cords. Their beads were traditionally used in many transactions, which included the building of new traditional structures, such as men's clubhouses, as well as (historically) the rewarding of head hunters or dancers. These beads are a symbol of rank and power within a family, and every possible effort is made to hold on to traditional bead money. Today, souvenir bead money can be found carved of wood or made from other synthetic materials.

Another type of traditional Palauan "money" is called a *toluk* (Figure 89). This is a tortoiseshell dish or plate, oval in shape, which has four or more small tabs sticking out on its sides like a turtle's legs or fishtails. Experts form these plates by pressing the shell of the hawksbill turtle into wooden molds. These plates continue to be made today and are used by women in traditional transactions such as marriages and funerals. Early visitors to Palau were often given *toluk* as gifts to show respect. *Toluk* are still available in gift shops on Palau today to the detriment of the hawksbill turtle, since not all countries have agreed to the restrictions of CITES.

FIGURE 89

Micronesian clubs, such as traditional "bull horn" spiked clubs from Chuuk (Figure 90), may still be produced today in limited quantities. However, the Republic of Kiribati is especially famous for its weapons and armor including swords, daggers, and tridents set with shark's teeth. Kiribati's spiked helmets are made from giant *diodon* or puffer fish, while body armor is woven from heavy, twisted coconut fiber. Such armor was worn in battle and included trousers and a collar-like extension that protected the back of the neck.

Dance paddles (Figure 93) were small paddle-like or club-like accessories that were used in traditional dances. They were originally produced in Palau, Chuuk, and Pohnpei, although they appear to no longer be produced on Palau. Pohnpei dance paddles are those most frequently encountered, as they are still being made today. They are made of a soft, light-colored wood such as breadfruit wood, which is painted black and then incised with geometric designs. Tufts of plant fiber ornament the sides of the paddle. Older paddles are generally larger, with a greater

WEAPONS, DANCE PADDLES, TOOLS, AND "LOVE STICKS"

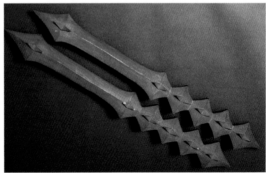

FIGURE 90

FIGURE 91

number of more closely spaced tufts, while, through simplification, later paddles are smaller and generally have fewer and more widely spaced tufts and less complex incised designs.

Traditional style adzes (Figure 91) set with shell blades are still found on Yap and its surrounding islands but are rarely used for carving and cutting today. They were once used in Palau, Chuuk, and throughout Micronesia since appropriate stone for adze blades were rarely available. Once westerners began to trade with Micronesian peoples, the shell adze blade was replaced by iron on most islands. Tridacna shell is traditionally used to form the cutting blade. Other weapons historically used in Micronesia included slings, spears, and bows and arrows.

Tools such as the shuttles for backstrap looms and sets of tattooing tools can be appreciated for the beauty and simplicity of their design. In early times, many Micronesian peoples, including those from the Marshall Islands, Yap, and Palau, wore distinctive patterns of tattoos, which were indicators of rank and status. The Yapese people were not allowed to practice tattooing during the Japanese times, although people in Ulithi continued the practice. Very few people have these tattoos today. However, at one time, on Yap and its outer islands, *yol* tattoos covering the chest, back, upper arms, and thighs were indicators of high caste or chiefly status, while *zalbachag* tattoos, which cover the lower legs, were the decorations permitted to a successful warrior. *Gachow* tattoos are a third category of tattoo. *Gachow* designs can be worn by men or women of any station, and each individual can choose his or her design (Untaman & Whitcomb 1956:71–74). Tattoo tools are still being made in Yap State. A tattoo adze has a wooden handle with a small-toothed blade made from bone attached at the end. This bladed tool is paired with a specially shaped hammer or mallet to tap the blade and, thus, mark the skin. Today, traditional tattooing in Yap and elsewhere has largely died out, although the recent popularity of tattooing in general may be fueling a revival of interest in Micronesians seeking connections to their historical pasts.

Another object produced on Chuuk is the "love stick." Such sticks (Figure 92), like dance paddles, appear to have originally been painted black and then incised with elaborate repetitive geometric designs. Kubary, the German ethnographer who was in Chuuk in 1877, described the courting sticks as having "at the four corners of the knob…attachments of piled up coconut rings or little plates between which small colored shell discs are inserted" (Kubary 1889:58). Over six feet long, the stick was notched and usually terminated in a rectangular, slightly tapering knob. The Krämer expedition in the early 1900s found detailed geometric designs, similar to those on love sticks, on houses, bowls, hair combs, dance paddles, and clubs. Different patterns had specific meanings referring to motifs that included fruits, birds, and fish (Krämer 1932:148–150, plates 13, 14). Love sticks were used by suitors to identify themselves. Each stick was different, and a young man would thrust his stick through the thatch of a young woman's house in the evening. If interested, she would pull the stick in; if not, she would push it back out.

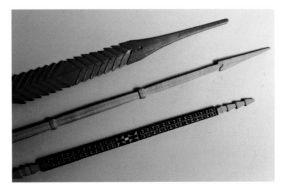

FIGURE 92

Identifying the stick in the dark was more about the shape of the stick itself, while the smaller patterns may have functioned to convey other messages during the day. Throughout the Japanese period, love sticks with elaborate incised designs remained popular. This style continued to be produced into the American period. In 1964, Angus McBean, in his book *Handicrafts of the South Seas*, describes the incised form of love stick as the most prevalent. "The most common type is about four feet long and one quarter inch square with highly detailed black and yellow geometric designs from the point nearly to the base. A second type is typically about two-and-a-half feet long, flat, and about three quarters of an inch wide, with carved detail in natural hard wood" (McBean 1964:103). This second style of unpainted stick with jagged carvings, which resemble and perhaps derive from Chuukese clubs, began to supplant the incised variety of love stick during the American period and is the only style of stick produced today. Interestingly, informants told anthropologist Frank Lebar, who was in Chuuk from 1947–1948, that these elaborate patterns were not used on love sticks before the

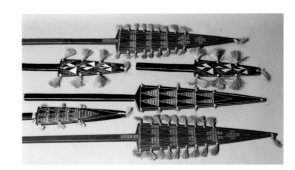

FIGURE 93

FIGURE 94

introduction of steel knives (LeBar 1964:180). This comment may have been meant to justify the production of plain sticks by implying that they were an earlier, somehow purer form. On the other hand, just as styles in western clothing change, love sticks may have undergone changes in style prior to colonial contact. Certainly, Kubary's early description of the love stick appears to exhibit features that later love sticks lacked, including rings of coconut and shell discs. It does seem unlikely, though, that an elaborate iconography of incised designs should have developed in response to the introduction of steel knives. However, just like the decorations on the Palauan *bai*, the availability of metal tools may have encouraged their elaboration.

While Japanese collectors may have preferred love sticks with incised designs, changing historic and market influences undoubtedly influenced the form of the love stick during the American period. Dr. James Nason of the Burke Museum in Seattle has suggested, "The whole point of complex carving designs was, as we know, to allow young women to distinguish one suitor from another. Tourists hardly needed that level of detail, so very plain love sticks began to be made. While some early, post-war handicraft pieces still had somewhat complex designs because makers believed, erroneously as it turned out, that most tourists or military personnel would appreciate them and want the real thing, it apparently was not long before the simpler pieces were produced for this market, as examples from the late 1950s and early 1960s show" (Nason 2009). Another change in the love stick was also associated with the switch to the plainer style—the width of the stick increased from one-quarter of an inch to, in some later examples, more than three-quarters of an inch wide. This new width was probably not as effective in covertly piercing the thatch of a young woman's hut and probably signaled the fact that the love stick was no longer being used for its traditional purpose. The love stick continues to be an important item in the history of the Chuukese people and an intriguing item for visitors, although the courting practice behind its production has faded away.

FIGURE 95

CHAPTER FOUR

Woven Ware
and Adornments

Using laboriously prepared plant fibers, Micronesian women continue to weave objects of beauty and cultural meaning, which also provide an important source of household income. In early times, women's creations provided the woven fabric of everyday life in the form of utility baskets, clothing, baby carriers, and personal adornments. The valuable fiber objects they wove held important cultural and ritual significance and were also used as sources of trade goods for exchanges between islands.

In the beginning of the twentieth century, the German presence had already begun to discourage the production of some components of traditional material culture, as when, for example, they banned the construction of the *bai* or men's house in Palau. In addition, the Japanese occupation of Micronesia, beginning in 1914, was associated with a tremendous increase in the number of Japanese immigrants. This influx of Japanese had a significant effect on the Micronesian economy. At that time, Japanese colonists outnumbered the indigenous people of Saipan, the Chamorro, nearly ten to one. The strong wage economy was primarily based on the development of plantations, fisheries, and phosphate mining operations (Yanaihara 1940:30). The islanders' demand for Japanese-manufactured products, such as tinned food and imported clothing, led to a decline in the production of traditional, woven products,

FIGURE 96

FIGURE 97

especially on major islands where there was access to wage labor and imported goods. However, the Japanese administration continued to encourage handicraft production, both to generate additional income and to preserve material culture. In fact, in 1929, the Japanese Civil Administration established a products museum in Palau to exhibit the characteristic styles of different island groups (Udui 1964:4). According to researcher Elizabeth Udui, they also set craft quotas and were even authorized to use such inducements as whipping to see that these quotas were met. Agricultural extension agents went to villages and taught additional handicraft techniques, including weaving, sewing, and the making of souvenirs such as coconut ashtrays. In the Marshall Islands, skilled women weavers were appointed to supervise the quality of the woven products (Udui 1964:4–5). As a result, today in the Marshall Islands, the Japanese word *amimono* is still used to describe handicrafts that are made exclusively for trade.

After WWII and in the early Trust Territory period, Micronesia was not open to tourism. Many handicrafts, including fans, baskets, and carvings, had initially been sold to military personnel. However, sales began to decline drastically during the period immediately after the war, since, once the area was secure, military personnel began to leave the islands (Udui 1964). It was not until Micronesian countries were opened to tourism in the mid 1960s that handicraft production once again became a significant source of income for the Micronesian economy. For example, in 1979, over 23,000 visitors to FSM spent $825,000 on handicraft items—an average expenditure of thirty-five dollars per person (Nason 1984:443). Much of this income was generated by women from the production of woven items. Micronesian women organized clubs and associations for the production of handicrafts. Woven ware has remained important to this day, especially in smaller, outer islands where, although wood for carving is in short supply, plant materials for fiber crafts are readily available. This continued economic activity has helped to preserve an amazing variety of weaving designs and techniques.

Grass skirts are often associated with Hawai'i; however, Hawaiian skirts actually consist of strips of plant fiber too wide to give the appearance of grass. As former director of the Bishop Museum Peter Buck pointed out, "Old time garments were plaited from the fiber obtained from the outer covering of banana trunks…. They were like the plaiting of mats on the inside, and…long strips covered the outer surface. Similar garments were made from *ti* leaves" (Buck, 1957:165). In contrast, "grass" skirts can be defined as skirts consisting of numerous, separate, grass-like strands, actually made from the fibers of one of a variety of plant species including coconut, hibiscus, and banana. Similar skirts were originally worn by women on islands such as Yap, Palau, and Kiribati as well as by men on Pohnpei. On other islands, woven skirts (*lava lava*) were used for clothing, and grass skirts were donned only for dances. Some Yapese women still wear grass skirts, which may weigh up to thirty pounds, although today they may wear a shirt instead of going topless. On Yap and outlying islands, it is still considered acceptable to bare your breasts but obscene to expose your thighs. During the 1950s, several types of Yapese skirts were made—everyday skirts, work skirts, and dance skirts. Everyday skirts were made from green leaves including betel nut leaves, banana leaves, coconut fronds, and ferns. Work skirts were made from browned banana leaves (Untaman and Whitcomb 1956:31–34). Dance skirts are still being made from hibiscus fibers in brightly dyed stripes. On Yapese skirts, a short outer fringe hangs to the hip line, while a longer under skirt extends below the knees.

Palauans also traditionally wore grass skirts, which consisted of two sections, front and behind, decorated with long twists of exceptionally thick fibers at the hip. According to author Ann Hillman Kitalong, Palauan women made approximately two dozen types of grass skirts (*cheriut*) including those from sedge, the *ti* plant, coconut fronds, banana leaves, the inner bark of the hibiscus, and other plants. Hibiscus twine held together the two panels of the skirt, which also included a pandanus pocket woven into the skirt and a woven belt with two triangular sections that hung down for modesty. Skirts were dyed in different colors

FIGURE 98

signifying a woman's rank and clan affiliation (Kitalong 1998:129). The skirt generally hung below the waist, while a tight belt, now often made from leather, encircled the waist. Grass skirts are rarely worn by Palauan women today, however, except for special celebrations like the First Childbirth Ceremony or for traditional dances.

On Pohnpei, men also wore grass skirts, while the women seem to have originally worn a sort of *lava lava*, which, by the twentieth century, was supplanted by a wrap-around skirt made of trade cloth. As late as the 1940s, Pohnpeian men still sometimes wore a sort of short grass skirt, usually over shorts. During the Trust Territory period, grass skirts continued to be woven on Pohnpei with macramé knotted designs hanging down from the waistband. These were used for dance performances and were sold as souvenirs. In Kiribati, women traditionally wore a grass dance skirt, which consisted of a series of overlapping layers of coconut fiber. In Kiribati and Tuvalu, one- to four-inch wide strips of pandanus leaves are added to the outside of coconut fiber grass skirts to provide decoration for dances. These strips provide an over layer, which only extends approximately ten to twelve inches down around the skirt. In Kiribati, this separate decorative piece of fiber strips consists of shorter, green, pandanus leaves overlapping longer, beige, dried pandanus leaves. In Tuvalu, however, the pandanus strips are brightly painted in traditional colors with geometric designs, which overlap dyed-red strips extending the length of the underlying grass skirt. These decorative strips may be attached to a separate belt, which can be added or removed, or the strips may be stitched into the waistband of the skirt as part of the skirt itself. In Tuvalu, colors for dying fibers are laboriously derived from natural materials on the island. Lime from burnt coral provides yellow, the bark of the *noni* tree gives red, and black comes from the *tongo*, or mangrove, simmered for days with rusting metal included as a fixer. New colors are always being sought wherever they can be found. For example, purple is derived from boiling carbon paper (Austin n.d.:4).

FIGURE 9

FIGURE 100

Interestingly, even where handmade clothing such as mats, grass skirts, or *lava lava* have been abandoned, a characteristic dance skirt is often still produced, usually with significant innovations in style. The dance skirt could be partly a response to the expectations of foreign visitors but, also, a way to retain cultural integrity and community focus. In the Yapese outer islands where *lava lava* are still worn, a light grass skirt is sometimes layered over the *lava lava* when preparing for a dance. In Ulithi, *lava lava* are worn by adult women, while very young children often go naked. Young girls wear grass skirts before they come of age. While in Ngulu, another outer island of Yap State, adult women wear grass skirts very similar to those found on Yap Island itself.

Up until the late nineteenth or early twentieth century, Marshallese women wore finely plaited, square mats decorated in geometric patterns (Figure 100), one mat in front and one wrapped forward from behind. Men also wore clothing mats that were pulled between the legs, as a sort of loincloth, secured by being tucked into a belt from the front and back leaving only the fronts of the thighs exposed. For more formal occasions, the mat was worn more like an apron wound around the body. Chiefs also wore grass skirts beneath their mats, which were thicker front and back but exposed the sides of the legs (Spennemann 1998). There has been a revival

in the making of these intricate traditional mats, and weavers have again begun to plait some of the complex patterns that have specific symbolic meanings. This movement reportedly started in November 2006 when Maria Kabua Fowler, a traditional leader and activist, and Dr. Irene Taafaki, director of the Marshall Islands campus of the University of the South Pacific, viewed mats at the Bishop Museum with the assistance of Mary Lou Foley. Workshops were then held with weavers who shared their knowledge of traditional clothing mat patterns, which can convey information regarding family rank, genealogy, wealth, and spiritual and religious beliefs (Yacoe 2008). Geometric motifs may represent elements of sea life such as fish or turtles and other familiar natural motifs. In her 1986 University of Hawai'i master's thesis, Linda Le Geyt, points out the possible association between tattoo designs and designs found both on mats and early Marshall Islands fans (Le Geyt 1986:193). However, in the Marshall Islands today *mu'umu'u* or westernized clothing is most often worn, although special grass skirts are designed for dance performances. During the Trust Territory period, Marshallese women wore a dance skirt made from new coconut fronds (*kimej*) with a waistband decorated in intricate geometric patterns. At the Ninth Festival of Pacific Arts in 2004, Marshallese women wore aesthetically designed costumes, which included a dress mat decorated with a woven geometric pattern and ending in a long, layered fringe of fiber. The upper chest was covered with a thick collar of fiber (probably *kimej*), which came nearly to the waist.

Throughout Micronesia, men wore loincloths, which are called *thu* in Yap. In Pohnpei, Kosrae, and Yap, these were made using thin woven strips of banana fiber, often decorated in intricate geometric patterns. Woven loincloths were still being used as trade items in the early twentieth century. To this day, in Yap, strips of hibiscus fiber are used to complete the effect, hanging down beneath the loincloth. Today, the loincloth itself generally consists of strips of cotton trade cloth. In Pohnpei, the loincloth was augmented with a short grass skirt that was later worn over shorts.

FIGURE 103

At the time of western contact, women were weaving *lava lava* on backstrap looms on atolls between Yap and Chuuk as well as on Kosrae and Pohnpei. The existence of this type of loom in Micronesia is thought to be proof of an early connection to islands in Southeast Asia where a similar loom is used. While women set up the threads for weaving the *lava lava*, men construct the components of the loom. *Lava lava* are generally made from cloth woven from banana fiber, and are approximately twenty inches wide and up to eighty inches long, often woven in striped patterns with eleven-inch fringes at each end (Figure 101). *Lava lava* were used as wrap-around skirts or tol (a Ulithi word for "skirt"), as well as a form of money in traditional exchanges. While natural fibers are

gradually being replaced by cotton, these traditional skirts are still being woven and worn, especially on islands near Yap, such as Fais and Fassarai, an islet of Ulithi. These islands are famous for their *lava lava* or *tur* (a term that actually refers to a garment made completely from banana fibers) (Mulford 1980:12). The intricately woven fabric known as *machi* is especially impressive. This densely woven sacred textile is similar in size to a *lava lava* but more elaborate. *Machi* were used as burial shrouds for chiefs and high-ranking men. They were also used as tribute in exchanges with the Yapese high island, where Yapese chiefs wore the *machi* as cummerbunds in conjunction with their ceremonial loincloths. *Machi* were also once used as inaugural robes in the investiture of high-ranking, outer-island chiefs. The incredible intricacy of the *machi*, with its tightly woven patterns in black, white, and red fibers, has remained unchanged for over one hundred years. *Lava lava* were also used as items of ritual exchange in marriages and funerals, as gifts of love and respect, and as a medium of barter. Both *lava lava* and *machi* are still produced today (Walsh and Walsh 1989:12–15).

By the twenty-first century, throughout much of Micronesia with the possible exception of the Yap State, traditional dress has been replaced by westernized clothing. The narrow band that was once woven for men as a loincloth or *thu* was already in severe decline in the early twentieth century and today is no longer being made. While many women on Yap wear shirts, some women on outer islands surrounding Yap still go topless wearing trade cloth or *lava lava* as wrap-around skirts.

In recent decades, the women of FSM including those on Chuuk, Pohnpei, and Kosrae, have become known for making appliquéd, cotton skirts in floral designs. The skirts are modern works in the tradition of bedspreads, pillowcases, and other such items made during missionary times. These contemporary skirts in cotton blends have elastic waists, and the bottom of the skirt is scalloped to accommodate the outline of the floral design. Unfortunately, Asian businesses within the islands have begun to import replica skirts, which have been mass produced overseas.

Issues of copyright such as this one will become more common as globalization results in the increasing activity of foreign nationals in Micronesian nations. However, today, the production of mats, *lava lava*, and other woven products continues to be a testament to the importance of women in Micronesian societies. Many of these products continue to be integral to island life and have value as items of economic and ritual exchange.

The Marshall Islands are justly famous for the quality and variety of their jewelry designs that are woven using fiber and shell products. Examples of early twentieth century Marshall Island necklaces are seen in many German museums today. A classic example from the Museum für Völkerkunde zu Leipzig is made from pierced, bead discs of red spondylus shell, white clamshell, and coconut beads with a complex, carved, shell pendant attached (Treide 1997: plates 43, 44). Since WWII, Marshallese necklaces, called *marmar*, are usually woven from *kimej* (fiber from new coconut fronds) and decorated with a variety of cowry shells. The shells used include tiger, money, gold ringer, and strawberry cowries. In many recent examples, the cowries have been individually pierced and attached using natural fiber. However, in the 1940s and 1950s, cowries were attached to the necklace by stuffing fiber into the aperture of the cowry, then using glue or stiffener to seal it in. Usually, a tuft of fiber hung down below each shell attached in this way. The tuft became smaller in later necklaces, but this attachment technique is still sometimes seen in contemporary examples, since it does not require laboriously piercing individual shells. Other shells such as white *alu* shells and "cat's eyes" are also used. Beginning during the post-war period and extending through the 1970s, fibers were often dyed in bright colors using commercial dyes. During the period when carbon paper was being used on typewriters, Marshall Islanders took used carbon paper and extracted the purple dye. This resulted in an attractive, bright purple color, which unfortunately fades over time with exposure to sun. Necklaces made today often employ natural colors, which contrast nicely with the cowry shells. Many

FIGURE 105

95

FIGURE 106

FIGURE 107

beautiful and stylish necklaces continue to be produced, reflecting the popular demand for Marshallese creative skills (Figures 105 and 108). In Kiribati, women are known for their unique, traditional necklace designs. One style has discs of white shells attached as a series of pendants to a fiber base of human hair (Austin 1988:8). In 1995, Takerei Russell of AMAK, a national women's craft cooperative (since dissolved), was unable to obtain this style of necklace. However, it appears that they were still sometimes being produced, perhaps mostly as a valued family heirloom. The plaited hair that forms the base for this and other styles of necklaces is called a *bunna* and was thought to provide protection against evil spirits. This necklace, called a *karaebari*, is decorated with discs from the conus shell and was worn during dances (*ruoia*) (Koch 1986:149, 158–160). Pohnpei and Kosrae produce necklaces using cowries and natural fiber similar to those found in the Marshall Islands. In Saipan, as well as on atolls in the Carolines such as Pulusuk and Lamotrek, Carolinians currently create and wear large, decorative collars woven in intricate geometric patterns made from tiny, solid-colored, glass, trade beads.

A traditional style of Yapese necklace has handmade, orange shell beads and ends in a large orange "tooth." The tooth is made from a type of shell that is only found in Palau, and the Yapese call this type of necklace a *zawey* (Untaman and Whitcomb 1956:79). These necklaces are rare and desirable and are considered another a form of money. Yapese women wear necklaces made of hibiscus fibers dyed black, which they knot and hang down like lanyards both in front and in back to signal reproductive maturity. Today, they often use cotton to make this necklace. For dances, they create special neck *lei*, which consist of a decorative fiber fringe generally dyed in a variety of colors attached to form wide bands of color. Originally, these *lei* were made entirely of arduously prepared natural fibers, but today synthetic materials are slowly replacing the natural fibers.[18] Transitional examples have a natural fiber fringe attached to a plastic woven base. Currently, examples are being sold that are completely made from synthetic fibers. The time and effort required to prepare natural fibers has caused artificial materials to become increasingly attractive to weavers.

FIGURE 108

With the exception of beautiful and elaborate tattoos, which continued to be worn into the early twentieth century, much of Micronesian body adornment was perishable and needed to be constantly renewed. Head *lei* and necklaces, created from fragrant blossoms or leaves, were worn for the moment. Palm fronds could be tied around arms, wrists, or ankles as dance decorations, which could be discarded once the dance was over. Only the more durable adornments such as shell beads, tortoiseshell combs, and plaited mats, which have survived in museum collections or can be seen in early etchings and photographs, give us some idea of how Micronesians appeared in early times.

Today, beautiful yet durable head *lei* are woven in the Marshall Islands (where they are known as *wut*) and in Pohnpei, Kosrae, and Kiribati. In the Marshalls, one mid twentieth century style of head *lei* often has a row of white *alu* shells, from the *melampus* family of snail shells. The *alu* shells protrude like a crown from a natural-colored, woven circlet, with an intricate geometric pattern highlighted in another color. Kiribati weavers produce similar *lei*, which use cowries and a plain, fiber circlet. But, while shell-decorated head *lei* are still created, head *lei* used by modern Marshallese in their own celebrations have recently started to be decorated with handmade flowers shaped from natural fibers, such as hibiscus or pandanus, which are attached to a circlet to give the appearance of a flowered head piece. Sometimes leaf shapes are also cut from natural fiber and added to increase the realistic shape of flowers, although these are not colored. Silk flowers and leaves may also be added. The creation of elaborate flowers, using techniques such as teneriffe lace making, is also being included in these modern head *lei*. These flowers are also used to decorate hats, purses, hair ornaments, and other items. According to researcher and former Alele Museum curator Carol Curtis, a woman named Takien invented these teneriffe flowers, made with *kimej*, at Ron Ron on Majuro Atoll after WWII (Curtis 1986:47).

FIGURE 109

Micronesian traditional dress often included a belt, which acted to secure a woman's skirt or *lava lava* or a man's loincloth. For a number of decades, women on Palau have used leather belts to cinch their waists for special events like the First Childbirth Ceremony. Belts are also woven from natural fibers to coordinate with skirts for dances or other celebrations. In the early 1900s, Germans observed Palauan belts consisting of double strands of coconut shell or tortoiseshell discs. A similar type of belt made of two rows of coconut discs called a *katau* or *kauroro* is still made in Kiribati and is worn above a second belt called a *taona n riri*, which is made of braided twine ornamented with white snail shells (*buro*) strung together. Other shells are also sometimes used, and at least five varieties of ornamental belts and other necklaces and sashes are made in Kiribati along similar lines (Koch 1986:147, 155–157). But, one of the most beautiful traditional belts in Micronesia was once worn on Chuuk and is still produced in the Central Carolines. These elaborate belts combined laboriously handmade black and white clamshell bead discs with thin tortoiseshell cross supports into elaborate checkered patterns (Figure 110). Such belts were traditionally worn by women to support their *lava lava* but were also used for trade and tribute to the high island of Yap where, today, they are sometimes worn by girls during dances. The few belts in this style that are left in the islands today are valued family heirlooms. In this 1950 photo, two young dancers from Ulithi are shown decorating their cheeks with turmeric (Figure 111). They are wearing traditional shell and coconut bead belts with thin grass skirts made of green leaves draped over their *lava lava*. In modern times, similar belts are being made using black and white glass beads to recreate the same pattern. One type of belt (*kannir*) is woven in the Marshall Islands using a woven base to which seeds, cowries, and other shells are attached in distinctive designs. A particular belt that comes from Likiep Atoll in the Marshall Islands is composed completely of money cowries, which are attached using fishing wire with knotted natural fiber at each end (Wells 1982:27). Another belt purportedly created for the tourist trade was introduced to Kapingamarangi from the Marshall Islands. This belt used strips of pandanus covered with specially prepared coconut fronds,

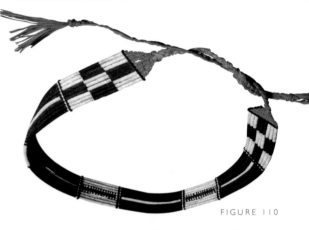

FIGURE 110

FIGURE 111

ornamented with the dyed outer skins of *puraka* stalks (a coarse dried taro), and overstitched with cowry shells (Buck 1950:275–278).

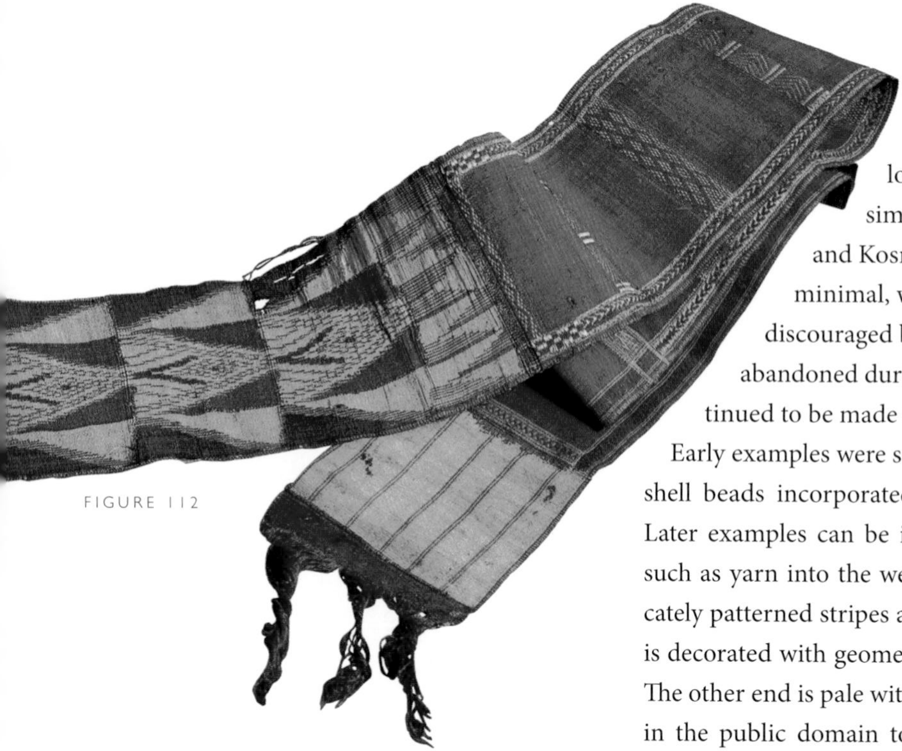

In Pohnpei, a finely woven textile called a *tor* was used as a sash mainly by high-ranking or prominent men. It was woven on a backstrap loom from banana or possibly hibiscus fiber. A similar textile known as a *tol* woven in both Pohnpei and Kosrae was worn as a loincloth by men and as a minimal, wrap-around covering by women. This style was discouraged by missionaries as too revealing and was largely abandoned during the nineteenth century. However, *tor* continued to be made into the first decade of the twentieth century.

Early examples were said to have had rows of pink, white, and grey shell beads incorporated into the weaving (Christian 1899a:289–290). Later examples can be identified by the inclusion of western materials such as yarn into the weave. The sash is generally a dark red with intricately patterned stripes at intervals. On this example, one end of the sash is decorated with geometric patterns on a pale background (Figure 112). The other end is pale with cross-cutting lines. These sashes are rarely seen in the public domain today, but many museums such as the Peabody Essex Museum in Massachusetts and the Metropolitan Museum in New York have excellent examples as part of their Micronesian collections.

In early times, the hair comb was an important decorative object for men on islands of Micronesia including the islands of Chuuk, Yap, and Palau. Decorative combs, made from wood or tortoiseshell, held men's hair, which grew long and was coiled into a bun. This coil was generally higher on the heads of men and at the nape of the neck in women. In western countries like Spain, women were the ones who wore elaborate hair combs. But, traditionally, women throughout Micronesia generally secured their long hair in a knot and wore flowers, head *lei*, and other adornments instead of combs. In Chuuk, men's combs protruded off to the side, from the top of the head, as an impressive ornament. Chuukese

FIGURE 112

men were especially known for their large ornamental comb designs, which included feathers, shells, and other decorative attachments. These combs complimented the wearer's enlarged ear lobes, which held heavy earrings consisting of tortoiseshell or coconut shell discs. Their combs were made by binding the teeth of the comb together using fibers and then attaching other ornaments. Chuukese combs were still being worn during German times. However, by the early twentieth century, they had been largely abandoned by Chuukese men. Today, Chuukese women are the ones who wear combs, which appear to be similar and possibly derived from western combs in style.

Palauans wore tortoiseshell combs during German times; however, this type of comb largely fell into disuse during the Japanese period and was replaced by pegged, wooden combs similar to those found in Yap (Matsumura 1918:113). In both Palau and Yap, the pegged, wooden comb was made of multiple pieces of mangrove wood that were pierced and, then, attached together using wooden "nails." Fibers were also sometimes used to attach the comb teeth (Figure 113). The Yapese word for comb is *rowey*, and pegged combs with "fixed teeth" are called *richib*. As defined in Untaman and Whitcomb, "This kind of comb is called *richib* in Yapese because *richib* means pin or nail" (Untaman and Whitcomb 1956:81). Into the mid-twentieth century, decorative, pegged combs were still being worn by men. The size and elaboration of these combs correlated with the wearer's social status, and certain groups in Yap were not permitted to wear these combs. During the Japanese period, ethnographer Matsumura pointed out, "Class system is strictly enforced in Yap, where even the wearing of ornaments is not permitted to everyone. There are consequently restrictions on the use of combs, free men alone are entitled to wear them, slaves being forbidden to use them or other ornaments under pains of heavy punishment…. The size of the comb differs…so that it will be seen that combs are worn in Yap not only for practical use and ornament but also as a mark of class distinction" (Matsumura 1918:112). The *richib* may have fallen out of use as these social distinctions lessened. Today, the elaborate, pegged combs are no

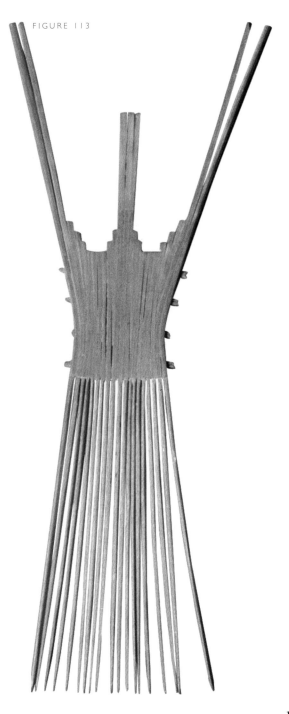

FIGURE 113

longer worn by men in Yap, but both men and women, usually from the older generation, use a form of this pegged comb as a utilitarian tool for grooming and lice removal. Today, few combs are worn by Palauans, but those that are would generally be worn by women. Palauan statuary, however, continues to depict the male figure wearing the comb.

A second style of comb known as a *yep* is still made throughout Yap today using thin, overlapping pieces of mangrove wood tied together using coconut or hibiscus fibers, which allow it to spread out like a fan (Figure 114). Today these *yep* are often adorned on the top with shavings of wood and are made by specialists using a unique, sharpened piece of shell. The *yep*, known as the "flowing" comb, is worn on the right, front side of the head usually by men from fourteen to fifty who are dressed for a dance.[19]

FIGURE 114

Today, many women on Chuuk, Kiribati, Tuvalu, and the Marshall Islands still grow their hair very long, twist it into buns, and wear modern-style hair combs. These are most commonly store-bought, plastic combs, which are wide and curved with many teeth. In the Marshall Islands, the plastic combs may be ornamented with woven flowers. Wooden combs with two to four prongs and a carved top consisting of a series of knobs or other ornament could be found on Chuuk in the 1990s, and such wooden combs are still being produced there today. Wooden combs are also being made and used on Woleai and Yap. In FSM, various islands also produced curved combs similar to the plastic ones, but made from real tortoiseshell with many teeth and a scalloped top (Rolls 1991:7, 36). Some handmade combs have been created from assimilated modern materials. For example, as late as the1960s, combs from Kiribati were being made from aluminum salvaged from WWII aircraft. Later, combs on Kiribati were made from PVC piping, typically with brightly colored words engraved on them. These were commonly produced by inmates from the women's prison. The combs act as identity markers to the extent that they may actually have "Kiribati" or another island name carved on them, although sometimes the name on a comb does not actually reflect the wearer's island of origin. Long hair is still considered customary for women throughout eastern Micronesia.

In the Marshall Islands and on Kiribati and Tuvalu, oval hair ornaments are made that are pierced with two holes for a stick to be thrust through, thus holding a bun or twist of hair in place. These can be woven from *kimej* and edged with *alu* shells, as in the Marshall Islands, or edged with money cowries, as on Kiribati and Tuvalu. This design is also sometimes made of tortoiseshell in Kosrae, Pohnpei, and Chuuk. In the Marshall Islands, women also make a series of creative hair sticks, which are designed to be pushed into a bun and to produce a decorative effect. The ends of these sticks are ornamented with woven leaves and flowers, silk flowers, seeds, and various woven ornaments. The art of hair adornment continues perhaps partly because it provides a distinctive focus for cultural identity.[20]

FIGURE 115

MARSHALL ISLANDS BASKETS, TRAYS AND PURSES

The Marshall Islands consist of thirty-three atolls, which cover a total area of approximately seventy square miles (Karolle 1988:41, 44). These islands have one of the highest populations of any Micronesian nation and, as of July of 2009, had an estimated population of 50,000 (RMI Embassy 2008). Two-thirds of the nation's population lives in two urban centers—Majuro, the capital, and Ebeye on Kwajalein Atoll. Since 1964, Kwajalein Atoll has been the home of a major U.S. military base. Currently, the U.S. Army operates the Ronald Reagan Ballistic Missile Defense Test Site there. Two Marshallese atolls, Bikini (Pikinni) and Enewetak (Eniwetok), were nuclear test sites from 1946 to 1958. Due to a long U.S. military history and presence, many finely woven craft items from the Marshall Islands, as well as crafts from throughout Micronesia, have been brought to the United States as souvenirs by military and civilian personnel on Kwajalein. The "Mic Shop" on the base has a selection of handicrafts from throughout Micronesia, including Palau, Chuuk, and Yap. This dispersal of handicrafts from multiple island origins can later result in confusion of provenance when, once again, the origin of an object is attributed to its point of purchase.

In her book, *Decorative Marshallese Baskets*, Judy Mulford asserts, "the Marshallese women are considered to be the finest and most productive basket makers in Micronesia" (Mulford 1991:11). In order to describe their mats, baskets (Figure 116), trays, and wall hangings, it is first necessary to understand the materials from which they are made. The majority of contemporary Marshallese plait work incorporates four major materials: *malwe*, *maan*, *kimej*, and cowry shells. *Malwe* is the central rib of the coconut frond, which has been scraped to the pithy core. *Maan* are sectional strips of pandanus leaves, which are generally wrapped around the *malwe*. New and dried pandanus leaves are used to create slightly different colors and effects. These two materials, after being wrapped together, are coiled to form the major components of mats, baskets, and wall hangings. The coils are attached using *kimej*, which is obtained from the new shoots of coconut palms. *Kimej* is also used to create decorative teneriffe lace designs, which are usually featured in the center and sometimes the sides of baskets, as well as in the interstices of wall hangings (Mulford 1991:20). Teneriffe was derived from an early European technique of lace making, which some think was introduced into the Marshall Islands by the Japanese (Mulford 1991:63). This basket-making technique also has many interesting parallels with a pine needle tradition of folk art basketry found in the United States that incorporates similar medallions of teneriffe but uses bundles of pine needles instead of pandanus.

The use of cowry shells in teneriffe baskets has become widespread, especially throughout eastern Micronesia. Generally, four types of cowry shells are used to edge mats, baskets, and wall hangings. They may also be used in combination with teneriffe designs in the center of baskets and wall hangings. Money and gold ringer cowries are most commonly used. Larger tiger cowries are occasionally included as accents (usually in mats and baskets from Pohnpei). Strawberry cowries are also used, although

FIGURE 116

usually reserved for necklaces. Marshallese plait work can sometimes be dated by observing the way in which cowries are attached to the borders of mats and other items. Woven Marshallese tablemats (trade mats, not clothing or utilitarian mats) are usually small and circular. Some very old examples, probably from the Japanese period or immediately after WWII, incorporate knotted decorative patterns into the tightly woven body of the mat. One mat, for example, actually has a design of bows imbedded in the neutral-colored fiber. In these oldest mats (1930s–1940s), just as in older necklaces, shells are placed wide end toward the mat, and they appear to be attached by stuffing binding fiber, probably *kimej*, into the cavity of the shell rather than piercing it. In more recent mats, from the 1970s to the present, the shells are positioned narrow end toward the mat and are neatly pierced and secured using *kimej*. This change in practice almost certainly reflects an increased availability of piercing tools in recent times. In baskets from the 1980s or 1990s, some cowries have been pierced and secured lying on their sides, perhaps to conserve cowry shells. Newer Marshallese mats sometimes have stripes of dyed fiber, while older mats often have a wide fringe associated with fiber issuing from the shell's aperture, where the fiber has been stuffed in and secured. Similar mats, which are produced in the Philippines, are readily identifiable by the use of synthetic fibers or bleached coconut fronds instead of *kimej*, less complicated weaves and teneriffe designs, unmatched shells, and more widely spaced cowries.

Trays are distinguished from baskets by being shallower and usually oval in shape. They are often larger than baskets, which are generally round. Marshallese baskets and trays are characteristically trimmed with cowry shells along their lip, while the sides are constructed of *malwe*/*maan* in strips, which are attached together with *kimej*. The majority of the design is in the floor of the basket or tray and consists of teneriffe designs or may exhibit other techniques such as looping. Looping is a form of knotless netting that acts as a filler for open areas in a teneriffe design. Teneriffe designs may be woven from *kimej* dyed in brilliant colors. Shells are added, and sometimes inserts of tortoiseshell are seen in

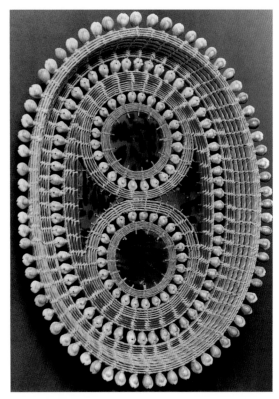

FIGURE 117

examples that predate the international ban on the import of tortoiseshell to the U.S. Floral or geometric designs predominate, but some trays even appear to depict scenes, such as trees reflected in water (Figure 118), shown in one example. Marshallese wall hangings are large, flat, and decorative. They make extensive use of the same materials used in Marshallese mats and baskets. Bright colors and complex patterns are utilized to create a decorative effect in teneriffe baskets. Baskets, wall hangings, and trays demonstrate the creative range of Marshallese weavers and the incredible scope and diversity of their designs (Mulford 1991, 2006).

Decorative baskets using teneriffe and cowry shells are also produced in Kiribati, Kosrae, and Pohnpei. Kiribati baskets and wall mats essentially exemplify the same techniques as do Marshallese baskets, except that their pandanus-wrapped bundles employ brightly dyed colors alternating with repeated rows of cowry shells starting at the rim of the basket, wall mat, or tray and continuing into the center. Also, as in most islands, traditional baskets for storage and transport are quickly woven from pandanus fibers. Tablemats and trays are ornamented by creating patterns with stitches using the lighter coconut fronds, which hold the coils of dark, wrapped pandanus leaves together. Kiribati weavers are especially known for their traditional, fine, baby mats, which are plaited on both sides to create geometric patterns by contrasting light and dark fibers. Kosraen weavers tend to make baskets and trays using darker selections of pandanus-wrapped bundles. Rows of cowry shells are used discretely, rarely on the rim of a basket, but sometimes around the inside of the rim or in the circular center. Most baskets are in natural colors, although some purses made to sell to tourists are being embroidered with patterns or scenes highlighted in bright shades of pink, green, and blue. Both Pohnpeians and Kosraens make beautiful, star-shaped Christmas ornaments. Kosraens use light fiber and shells on their stars, while Pohnpeians tend to contrast dark fibers with light shells.

Pohnpei specializes in wall mats and shallow baskets or trays. Cowries are not used to ornament the outer rim but are often incorporated within the border in conjunction with a zigzag pattern of thin, pandanus-wrapped bundles. The center of these baskets or trays often includes a woodcarving of sea creatures, such as dolphins or sharks, or perhaps a large shell, which has a floral design made of small shells that are glued onto it. In mats created prior to the 1975 ban, a circular piece of tortoise-shell was sometimes pierced and fixed in the center.

Palauans are known more for their woodcarving than their plait work. Nevertheless, they produce interesting woven items, mostly for practical, everyday use. Their primary plaited products are woven clutch bags called *tets*. Palauans use *tets* to store their betel nut chew and other personal effects. *Tets* lack handles and contain a plain inner liner. They are used by Palauans but are also sold to tourists, along with larger more purse-like versions that do have handles. Inside tets, Palauans keep a pouch, woven from pandanus or coconut fibers, the size of an eyeglass case called a *blia kebui* to store the leaves some Palauans use to wrap their betel nut chew. The majority of these baskets use dyed

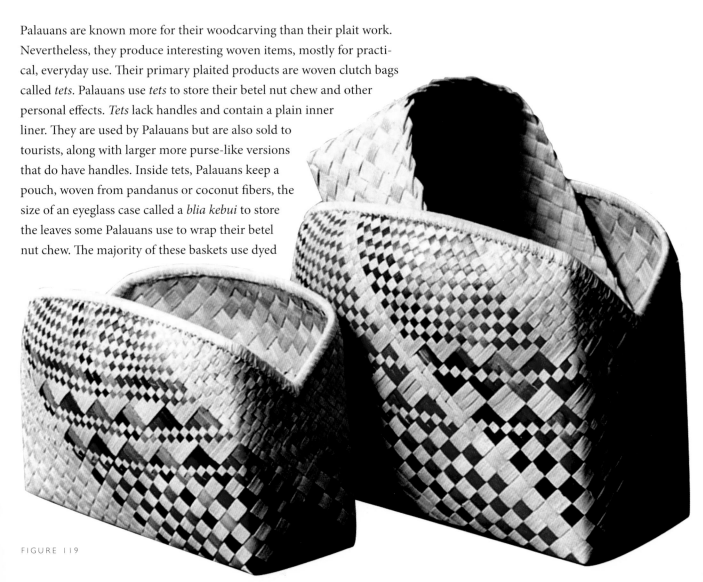

FIGURE 119

FIGURE 120

strips to create geometric designs in colors such as green and purple. In the more purse-like versions, cowry shells are used to create a closure with the help of a pandanus loop. Other Palauan baskets are made including large food baskets, fishing baskets, and baskets used to hold cooked starches like breadfruit and taro (Kitalong 1998:129).

A classic style of box-shaped purse is produced in the Marshall Islands, Kosrae, and Kiribati. The techniques of construction are so similar that, without knowing the provenance of the purse, it is sometimes hard to differentiate them. The purse incorporates darker or dyed fibers to create the geometric designs used in traditional mats against a neutral background of pandanus (Figure 120). The purse has a woven handle and a shell closure and is lined in plain woven pandanus. Sometimes in Kiribati, pieces of very old mats are actually used in the construction of these purses. Marshallese examples incorporate pieces of tortoiseshell, as well as shells or teneriffe, into the walls of the purse. A unique, box-shaped purse is produced in the Marshall Islands called a "Kili Bag" (Figure 121). These purses have two handles and a fitted lid that comes down snuggly to close the purse. This purse exceeds all others in the quality and tightness of its weave. Bikini (Pikinni) Islanders who were displaced by nuclear testing were settled on Kili in the Ralik Chain of the Marshall Islands. Kili has no lagoon, so one of the few ways that the community could earn money was by constructing these fine bags from *kimej*. The Kili Bag was made famous when Jackie Kennedy carried one during the 1960s.

The Yapese weave a traditional purse called a *waey* to carry their betel nut chew. A fringe of decorative fibers hangs down beneath the purse (Figure 122). Nearly everyone on Yap carries a *waey* under his or her arm, since these bags have no handles. The Yapese also weave several other practical baskets including one for carrying a baby.

Carolinians in Saipan, as well as Chamorros on Guam, crocheted a selection of attractive handbags that were decorated with different shades of an indigenous land snail, the fat Guam partula (Figure 123). This snail

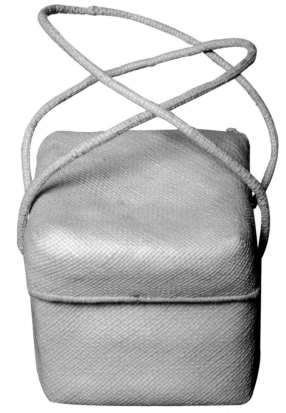

FIGURE 121

comes in white, light brown, and a salmon pink. Crochet thread was used to form the base of the purse to which the snail shells were attached in a variety of patterns. The purses were generally lined in a silken or rayon fabric and sometimes incorporated western features such as metal zippers. The production of these purses, using the easily gathered land snails, during the 1940s, 1950s, and 1960s greatly endangered the fat Guam partula, and these purses are not made today.

The production of baskets, trays, purses, mats, and other woven items is a vital cultural and economic activity in Micronesia. Though different groups may exchange ideas, each island has its own characteristic style. However, one type of basket that is found in a similar form throughout Micronesia is the utility basket. A utility basket is a practical basket woven quickly to function as a container. Palm fronds are requisitioned as the need arises, and a useful basket is made to accommodate the needs of the moment to carry fruit, for example, or whatever may be required. Clearly Micronesian baskets continue to be important as functional objects as well as creations of beauty and inspiration.

FIGURE 122

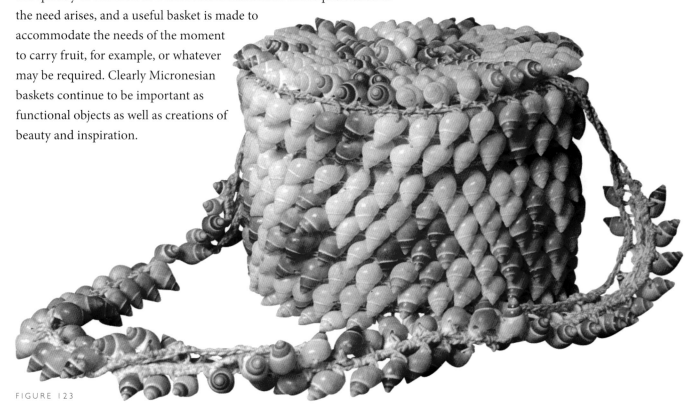

FIGURE 123

Hand fans provide a fascinating and varied arena for the cross-cultural comparison of Micronesian material cultures. Nearly every island group has its own characteristic style of hand fan, and some produce several different styles associated with different functions, traditions, or provinces. Historical relocations, as a result of droughts or hurricanes as well as the intervention of colonial administrators or missionaries, have all resulted in the introduction of new fan styles. In 1994, weavers on Kosrae advised Peace Corps worker Jeannie Latenser that a style of fan called *pal tok* or "sunburst" was introduced by Marshall Islanders who were brought to Kosrae by the Japanese shortly before WWII. Another Kosrae fan was called *pal malem*. The word "*pal*" means "fan," and the word "*malem*" refers to the Malem municipality in Kosrae where the fan is made (Figure 124). The intricate patterns woven on the face of the *pal malem* fans were said to replicate traditional patterns in men's clothing. Linda Le Geyt, in her thesis "Hand Fans of Micronesia," identified an example of a *pal malem* style fan dating back to 1936 recorded as collected on Yap (Le Geyt 1986:113–114). Three other examples were collected—one in 1965 in the Mokil district of Pohnpei, one in 1966 in the Marshall Islands, and another in 1966 in Kosrae (Le Geyt 1986:143, 156, 159). The examples shown here (Figure 124) were made in 1994 by Kosrae weavers Jada Joseph and Mary Moses. The issue of fan identification is complicated by the fact that the stated island of origin of a particular fan in museum records is not always accurate, since the island where the fan was found does not always reflect where the fan was made. Another style of fan, which author Marjorie Wells identifies as a "Kosrae style" fan (Wells 1982:108) is documented in five examples by Le Geyt. Of these, two were documented as collected on Kosrae, one on Namoluk Atoll (part of the Mortlock Islands), and two from the Marshall Islands (Le Geyt 1986:122, 156, 159, 217, 223). Kosrae weavers were shown a photo of a "Kosrae" fan in 1994 (Figure 125). Three older weavers recognized it, and one weaver offered to make an example. She was not sure if the fan she was shown was intrinsically a Kosrae style or, like the *pal tok*, was borrowed from another

FIGURE 124

FIGURE 125

island such as the Marshalls. She said, "All styles of fan are used by everyone now." Certainly, identical fan styles are often recorded as collected on different islands and may, as the *pal tok* example (Figure 126), reflect the movement of weavers from one island to another.

Le Geyt obtained numerous photographs of Micronesian hand fans from museum collections around the world during the course of her research. Most of the two hundred and ten fans she studied dated from the early 1900s through 1986. She dealt with fans attributed to different political regions separately, identifying some styles as pan-Micronesian while emphasizing the influences of traders, missionaries, and contacts between residents of different islands as an explanation for the presence of identical fan styles on different atolls. She also observed, as shown earlier, that "completely different shapes and constructions of fans can exist contemporaneously and were accepted. Perhaps it is also true that some fans were crafted for the social elite [in Kosrae], or that they were given as special gifts or used as items of trade" (Le Geyt 1986:153–154).

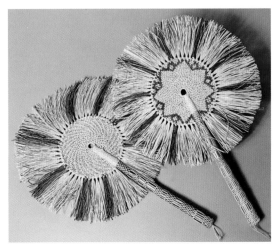

FIGURE 126

Hand fans functioned as an important item for exchange along with intricate mats, *lava lava*, and other woven items. Retired Captain Walter Karig, U.S. Navy, was in Micronesia immediately after WWII and was one of the early military personnel to enter the remote atolls to render assistance. In his book *The Fortunate Islands*, he observed that, when visiting an atoll anywhere in Micronesia, "You will be crowned with chaplets of shells, presented with a beautifully woven fan, or if you appear to be of chieftain status, with a fan of tortoiseshell and feathers" (Karig 1948: 46) (Figure 132). As Karig prepared to leave Mokil Atoll, he described a parting exchange, "To the chief, I gave an impressive and coveted pair of sunglasses and he gave me a pair of regal fans, really badges of nobility more than utilitarian breeze stirrers or fly whisks" (Karig 1948:172). Karig's comments suggest that, even immediately after WWII, ornamental fans were still given as a sort of tribute from islanders to visitors. Linda Le Geyt also documents another such occurrence on Kosrae. Dr. Yoshio Kondo, a member of the 1936 Bishop Museum expedition, was gifted a "Kosrae style" fan by King Sigrah of Kosrae (Le Geyt 1986:153). Similarly, other woven items have traditionally been used for trade or tribute between islands or as gifts to special visitors. Interestingly, the earliest fans in Le Geyt's sample did not have teneriffe designs or feather decoration. These elaborations may have been introduced during the Japanese period of craft production.

Fire fans are some of the earliest documented fans, found in nearly every Micronesian island group. All are quite similar but have slight but distinctive differences in their weave and construction depending on their island origin. Fire fans were one of the most common categories of fans collected during the German period. These ubiquitous fans are used as tools to aerate embers and get a fire started. Quickly and simply constructed from available materials, they are often just as easily singed and discarded. Made from a single palm leaf, the construction technique used on specific islands appears to have changed little through the course of the twentieth century. For example a particular style of Kiribati fan called a kakako or "fresh palm leaf" was made in the 1990's in a form almost identical to an example documented as collected in 1889 (La Geyt 1986:235-236). The fire fan illustrated here (Figure 127) was collected in Palau in 2004.

FIGURE 127

Islands such as Pohnpei and Kosrae have as many as four or more distinct fan styles. But Marshall Islanders appear to have the greatest variety of styles of fans as well as the greatest variation in designs within those styles. One of the earliest documented Marshall Island fans (Figure 134) has decorated woven borders with designs similar to those found on Marshall Islands clothing mats and tattoos. Examples of this style can be found in most major Micronesian museum collections. These fans generally had a fan face which was square, round or oval with variations in the elaborate border and handle designs. The Marshallese word for fan is deel and the word deelel means "to fan" and also "a dance using fans" (Abo et al. 1976:354). The existence of this word implies a traditional Marshallese fan dance. Travelers Jemetha and Robert Cosgrove witnessed such a dance in Bouj Village, Aerok Island, Ailinglaplap Atoll on

March 17, 2003. Interestingly the fans used in this dance were decorative variations of the very early style with decorated woven border described above. They recorded their experiences in an online travel journal: "The women slowly shuffled and turned their way into a large moving circle, waving their fans and singing…. As the dance came to an end, the women took their turns removing their woven hats, fans and shell jewelry and left it in a pile before the *Irooj*, high chief or king" (Cosgrove and Cosgrove 2007). This account echoes earlier descriptions of the use of fans as a form of tribute and reaffirms a novel use of fans as dance accessories.

FIGURE 128

Le Geyt classifies fan types by the shape of the fan's face, including such categories as triangular, deltoid, truncated lozenge, circular, semi-circular, ovate, obovate, truncated obovate, rectangular, ovoid, and elliptical (Le Geyt 1986:50–66). Obovate-shaped fans continue to be extremely popular in the Marshall Islands (Figure 128). Contemporary Marshall Islands obovate fans usually have a floral design on their face executed in teneriffe and dyed with bright colors. The fan face can be edged with a fiber fringe or feathers. The oldest fans Le Geyt documents do not appear to have been decorated with feathers. Although feathers may have been originally present on some early examples and later deteriorated, it is more likely that the popular use of feathers to decorate fans today simply represents a change in fan styles that took hold during the twentieth century.

FIGURE 129

The handles of classic, mid twentieth century Marshall Island fans often consist of a piece of wood with a square end, which narrows roughly like an elongated pyramid toward the face and is covered with woven designs of variable intricacy. Other fans may have fibers gathered together in a bundle and then covered with a complex woven design to form the handle. Out of a selection of over seventy-five fans owned by the author, twenty different handle designs were identified. The Marshall Islands had the most variety with twenty-two fans and thirteen handle designs; Pohnpeian fans also had much variety with twenty-two fans and eight handle designs. While fans produced today are often of excellent quality, simplification has occurred, and fan handle designs are not as complex or finely woven as they once were.

One style of Pohnpeian hand fan is usually recognizable by its circular face, which is decorated with a fringe of feathers or fiber fringe in alternating colors. Older fans generally have a round insert of tortoiseshell, while modern versions of this fan are decorated inside using cowry shells rather than teneriffe designs. The handles of Pohnpeian fans are slightly longer and more rounded than Marshall Islands fans and are often more simply decorated with a weave consisting of the alternation of two contrasting colors. Pohnpeians also produce their own version of *pal tok*, as well as a diamond-shaped hand fan. Diamond-shaped hand fans are a pan-Pacific style that, with some variations, is still being produced on Pohnpei, Kosrae, Chuuk, and Guam and in the Marshall Islands.

FIGURE 130

The use of tortoiseshell in the face of a fan was traditionally associated with prestige and status. A fan in the Bishop Museum collection, in which the face consisted of a large piece of tortoiseshell, was collected in 1889. This fan was recorded as being owned by Chief Ligeri, a half brother to a high chief, or *irooj*, of the Marshall Islands (Le Geyt 1986:220–222). The use of tortoiseshell inserts in fans seems to have peaked in the period from the 1940s through the 1960s. Prior to the ban on the importation of the shell of the hawksbill turtle in 1975, fan production flourished, and fans often included square, round, and heart-shaped inserts of tortoiseshell incorporated into elaborate teneriffe designs.

FIGURE 131

Like many other items of handicraft in Micronesia, some examples of hand fans exemplify the process of material assimilation. This is not a new phenomenon but, instead, has gone on for over one hundred years. Islanders were quick to recycle or find unique uses for wool, cotton, ribbon, or other fabrics imported by foreigners. For example, Le Geyt describes one fan from Pohnpei dating to 1886 (fan number 178), which incorporates a flat band of red wool and a black cotton binder sewn on separately with fine twill to augment the raised border of the fan face

FIGURE 132

(Le Geyt 1986:134, 136–137). The preparation of natural fibers is highly labor intensive, and examples of some Pohnpei fans from the 1990s have even been found to incorporate strips of white plastic (Figure 130) into the weave of the fan face, possibly because such materials are easier to obtain and prepare. Fans from the Marshall Islands are occasionally seen with floral and other designs embroidered onto their faces in colored yarn. While the incorporation of modern materials occurs in a variety of contexts, it is far from supplanting the use of natural materials. Most fans today are still made entirely without the inclusion of such found materials.

According to Peace Corps worker Jeannie Latenser, in 1994, fans made on Kosrae were only being woven by older women. The youngest weaver was sixty-eight at that time. Younger people were not learning to produce the most finely woven and complex styles of fans, perhaps partially because less expensive and less authentic imported fans had become available in local shops. However, beautiful fans are still made throughout Micronesia. The sheer number of different styles of fans produced by individual island groups, including groups on Kosrae, Kiribati, and Pohnpei, and, of course, in the Marshall Islands, is a testament to the creativity of Micronesian weavers. Each of these island groups continues to weave several different styles of fans. Some fan styles have remained substantially unchanged for over one hundred years. For instance, a style of Kiribati fan called *nikunous* was collected in Kiribati as early as 1898 (Le Geyt 1986:240–241) and is produced today in virtually identical form. Other fan styles incorporate new materials, dyes, and techniques in an ongoing elaboration of this pan-Pacific art form, which also finds expression in Polynesia and Melanesia.

The fan-making tradition has continued to thrive but now operates in the context of a cash economy. Like other Micronesian crafts, as the process of globalization escalates, fan production is being threatened by competition from cheaper imports. But historically, the art of fan making has been one of the most vibrant and creative arenas for the fiber arts in Micronesia. Though some of the styles of fans shown here have already been discontinued, other styles are still being developed and continue to be elaborated. In some ways, the vitality of Micronesian hand fans reflects the creative energy that is part of all Micronesian handi-crafts—trading with tradition into the new millennium.

FIGURE 133

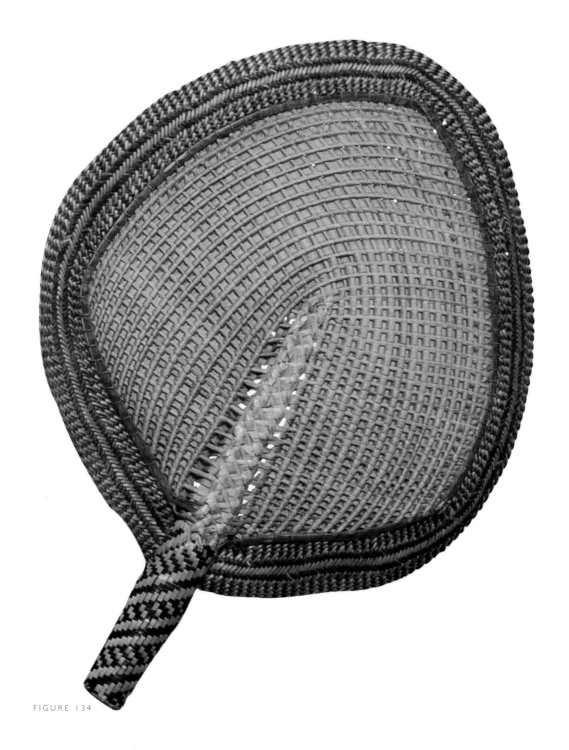

FIGURE 134

FIGURE 135

The people of Micronesia have always been traders. While their material culture has evolved as an adaptation to specific island environments, with the creation of such practical items as fish traps, utility baskets, and outrigger canoes, there has always been the need to develop unique, culturally meaningful items for exchange. Within island communities, alliances, funerals, marriages, and other celebrations often require the provision of food and the exchange of ritual valuables. Trading between neighboring islands separated in the vast Pacific ensured that basic resources would always be available in times of drought or hurricanes. In addition, trading with the "tall ships" that came from far away provided many commodities, such as metals, not found in Micronesia. By trading such objects, the many peoples of Micronesia have been able to promote and perpetuate their cultural traditions, while mediating their increased exposure to a global society. Despite the susceptibility of these islands to the incursions of disease and conquest, Micronesian arts and handicrafts and the artisans who produce them have remained resilient, creative, and adaptive.

This work has focused on Micronesia during a specific window of time—the twentieth century—and examined how historic forces have acted to modify artistic production, while documenting how unique, handcrafted objects have retained, throughout the decades, a cultural identification with their islands of origin. This research project has attempted to catalog the elements of material culture, which have been the focus of trade during this period, not only to identify and describe these objects but also to understand how they have changed and evolved in the context of changing cultures.

The creation of this book has been a long and interesting journey. This project began with the accumulation of a study collection that grew through the years, augmented by information gathered from many sources. It was often quite a challenge to find the necessary information about Micronesian handicrafts in print, and it is hoped that this work has helped to remedy the situation by bringing together many disparate sources. A number of people have played an important role in the creation of this book, including those who have shared their own experiences in the islands. It is hoped that the objects documented here will promote the appreciation and understanding of this richly creative and productive area of our world.

FIGURE 136

[1]This information was obtained from Peace Corps worker Jeannie Latenser, who was working with Kosrae women as part of the Kosrae Craft Project in 1994.

[2]The islands of Micronesia are small, and the volume of crafts they can produce has always been limited. Older and, thus, often more authentic Micronesian souvenirs are becoming harder and harder to find. These rare relics of the immediate post-WWII era appear very sporadically in rummage sales, garage sales, flea markets, and on eBay, usually only after a long determined search. Dealers in ethnographic art occasionally obtain early examples of statues or outrigger canoe models. However, fans, baskets, storyboards, and many other crafts are still being produced in the islands today, and, in most cases, the quality remains high. Most islands have one or more craft shops, which sell quality crafts directly to visitors. Obtaining crafts through mail order or the internet can be more challenging. In preparing this book, an attempt was made to update resources available to obtain handicrafts through the internet. Some individuals from Micronesian nations occasionally list contemporary crafts on eBay. The Yap Art Studio and Gallery has an easy-to-search website that provides information on crafts and quickly responds to inquiries and purchases.

[3]Eugenia Samuels, with the Micronesian Seminar, has an uncle who is a master carver on Chuuk. She was able to provide the information regarding Kuttu style statues being produced on Fefan.

[4]This information was obtained through email communication with Verna Curtis in 1995.

[5]This information was obtained through email communication with Lonnie Fread, manager of the Yap Art Studio and Gallery, in January of 2003.

[6]Hera Ware Owen administrated the Belau National Museum for over twenty years during the Trust Territory period.

[7]Information regarding Ululimar was provided courtesy of Kathleen Montvel-Cohen, who has a pair of squatting figures with characteristic facial features attributed to Ululimar.

[8]Thank you to Ronald Mayo, son of Frankie Mayo, who lived on Chuuk as a teenager from 1950 to 1957. He donated the pair of Kuttu statues shown in Figure 29 and substantiated their provenance.

[9]The substance commonly referred to as "tortoiseshell" is taken from plates that form the shell of the hawksbill sea turtle, an endangered species. The Convention on International Trade in Endangered Species of Wild Fauna and Flora (CITES) enacted a ban on all international trade involving this species in 1975. All items discussed in this book that are actually made from the turtle's shell will from now on be referred to as "tortoiseshell," since this is common usage.

[10]Hijikata Hisakatsu was a sculptor and artist who studied at the Tokyo School of Fine Arts. In 1929, he left the port of Yokohama for the islands of Micronesia. In Palau, he taught sculpture in the island schools, spending approximately two to three months at each school while recording observations about Palauan culture. After two and a half years, he moved to Satawal to continue his ethnological research in a more remote setting. After seven years, he returned to Palau where he collected ethnological materials as an official of the South Seas government. He returned to Japan in 1942. He was not only instrumental in training storyboard carvers and promoting the production of storyboards on Palau, but his ethnological researches, now published in a four-volume set, have also proved to be an invaluable resource (Hijikata 1991:20–27).

[11]Information on these carvings and the circumstances surrounding their production was obtained through email communication with James Nason on February 2, 2006. Additional information was also provided by Mac Marshall in a November 3, 2005 email.

[12]German texts, such as Krämer's, use "*galid*," while Kubary uses "*kalith*." A third term, "*chelid*," is used by Hijikata Hisakatsu and appears to be the currently accepted term. These three words are most likely cognates or interpretations of the same Palauan word.

[13]While Tobi Island is known as Hatohobei today, the term "*Tobi*" will be used for the remainder of this section, since all historical material discussed here uses the older term.

[14]All page numbers cited for Eilers are based on numbers supplied in parentheses on the manuscript pages of the HRAF translation from the German. Hopefully, these numbers coincide with the original German volume. I have not cited the page numbers of the translation itself, since different versions of the translation may have had different numbering.

[15]This information was based on personal communication with Leoncia Sims, a Palauan whose father had many contacts with Tobians in 1995.

[16]When Dr. Peter Black was on Tobi as a Peace Corps worker in 1968, he uncovered the figure mentioned in the text. He is now a retired professor of anthropology at George Mason University who runs a website entitled Friends of Tobi Island, which provides information about many aspects of Hatohobeian (Tobian) culture.

[17]Explanation of the greater value for *yar* that have been broken off on the sides was provided by Lonnie Fread, manager of the Yap Art Studio and Gallery in a January 2003 email.

[18]Celia Cords, a Yapese woman married to an American serviceman, met the author while her husband was stationed in Florida in 1996. She provided information regarding changes in the use of fibers in the production of Yapese necklaces.

[19]Thanks to Lonnie Fread of the Yap Art Studio and Gallery for using informants on Yap to verify Untaman and Whitcomb's distinction between *yep* and *richib*. Montvel-Cohen reverses the definition of these terms in his doctoral thesis.

[20]Information on the current use of hair combs in Micronesia came from an exchange with a group of anthropologists on the ASAONET list serve. Thank you goes out to Drs. Susanne Kuehling, Nancy Pollock, Sue Rosoff, Peter McQuarrie, Craig J. Severance, Laurence Carucci, Timothy Sharp, Mike Roman, Keith Chambers, and Mac Marshall.

Abo, Takaji, Byron W. Bender, Alfred Capelle, and Tony DeBrum. (1976). *Marshallese English Dictionary*. Pali Language Texts. Honolulu: University of Hawai'i Press.

Adelbai, Samuel Adiba, and Phyllis Koontz. (1972). The storyboards of Ngiraibuuch. *Guam and Micronesia Glimpses*: Second Quarter: pp. 24–29.

Advameg. (2010). Republic of Palau. *Encyclopedia of the Nations*. http://www.nationsencyclopedia.com/economies/Asia-and-the-Pacific/Palau.html. (February 9, 2010).

Alkire, William H. (1972). An introduction to the peoples and cultures of Micronesia. *Addison-Wesley Module*. no. 18. pp. 1–56.

Alkire, William H. (1989). *Lamotrek Atoll inter-island socio-economic ties*. Prospect Heights: Waveland Press.

Anonymous. (1949). *Arts and crafts of the Trust Territory of the Pacific Islands*. Guam: Division of Education, Education Press.

Austin, R. S. (1988). *Handcrafts of Kiribati*. Tarawa: Ministry of Trade, Government of Kiribati.

Austin, R. S. (1993). *The handcrafts of the Marshall Islands*. Suva: Forum Secretariat.

Austin, R. S. (n.d.) *The handcrafts of Tuvalu*. Suva: Fiji Times.

Black, Peter W. (1979). The Tobi stone figurine. Appendix 7: Tobi Stone Artifacts. Archaeological Test Excavations, Palau Islands. *Micronesica: journal of the University of Guam*. Douglas Osborne, ed. Supplement no. 1. Mangilao: University of Guam Press.

Buck, Peter H. (1950). *Material culture of Kapingamarangi*. Bulletin 200. Honolulu: Bishop Museum Press.

Buck, Peter H. (1957). *Arts and crafts of Hawai'i*. vol. 5: clothing. Special Publication no. 42. Honolulu: Bishop Museum Press.

Burrows, Edwin Grant. (1963). *Flower in my ear: arts and ethos of Ifaluk Atoll*. Seattle: University of Washington Press.

Buschmann, Rainer F. (1996). Tobi captured: converging ethnographic and colonial visions on a Caroline Island. *Isla: a journal of Micronesian studies*. 4:2. Dry Season. pp. 317–340.

Butler, Brian, ed. (1995). *Archaeological investigations in the Achugao and Matansa areas of Saipan, Mariana Islands*. Micronesian archaeological survey report no. 30. Saipan: Division of Historic Preservation.

Carlier, Jean-Edouard. (2007). Arts primitifs, curiosities, livres anciens. *Micronésie et Para-Micronésie*. Paris: Voyageurs et Curieux.

Christian, F. W. (1899a). On Micronesian weapons, dress, implements. *Journal of the Anthropological Institute of Great Britain and Ireland*. no. 28. London: Royal Anthropological Institute of Great Britain and Ireland. pp. 288–306.

Christian, F. W. (1899b). *The Caroline Islands: Travel in the sea of the little lands*. London: Methuen and Company.

Clark, Eugenie. (1953). *Lady with a spear*. New York: Harper and Row.

Cosgrove, Jemetha Clark, and Robert Cosgrove. (2007). The Marshall Islands. *Bazaar planet*. www.bazaarplanet.com/micronesia_index.html. (June 7, 2009).

Curtis, Carol. (1986). *Handicrafts of the Marshall Islands*. Unpublished manuscript. Majuro: Alele Museum.

Damm, Hans, and Ernest Sarfert. (1935). Inseln um Truk. vol. 2: Puluwat, Hok, und Satawal. *Ergebnisse der Südsee-Expedition 1908–1910*. G. Thilenius, ed. II, B, vol. 6, xxiii. Hamburg: Friederichsen, De Gruyter and Company.

Edge-Partington, James. (1890). *An album of the weapons, tools, ornaments, articles of dress, etc. of the natives of the Pacific Islands*. vols. 1, 2, 3. Issued for private circulation by James Edge-Partington.

Eilers, Anneliese. (1936). Westkarolinen: Tobi und Ngulu. *Ergebnisse der Südsee- Expedition 1908–1910*. G. Thilenius, ed. II, B, vol. 9, ii. Hamburg: Friederichsen, De Gruyter and Company.

Feldman, Jerome, and Donald H. Rubinstein. (1986). *Art of Micronesia*. Honolulu: University of Hawai'i Art Gallery.

Fischer, John L., Saul Riesenberg, and Marjorie G. Whiting. (1977). *The book of Luelen. Pacific series*, no. 8. Honolulu: University of Hawai'i Press.

Force, Roland M. (1959). Palauan money: some preliminary comments on material and origins. *Journal of the Polynesian Society*: 68. pp. 40–44.

Fraser, Douglas. (1962). *Primitive art*. New York: Doubleday and Company.

Fraser, Sir James George. (1968). The belief in immortality and the worship of the dead. *The belief among the Micronesians*. vol. 3. London: Dawsons of Pall Mall.

Fritz, Georg. (1904). The Chamorro: a history and ethnography of the Marianas. Elfriede Craddock, trans. Berlin: Ethnologisches Notizblatt. pp. 25–100.

FSM (Federated States of Micronesia population and housing census report for 2000). (2002). FSM Department of Economic Affairs.

Gilliland, Cora Lee C. (1975). The stone money of Yap: a numismatic survey. *Smithsonian studies in history and technology*. no. 23. Washington, D.C.: Smithsonian Institution Press.

Girschner, Max. (1911). Die Karolineninsel Namoluk und ihre bewohner. *Bassler Archiv*. vol. 2. pp. 123–215.

Goodenough, Ward. (2002). *Under heaven's brow: Pre-Christian religious tradition in Chuuk*. Philadelphia, PA: American Philosophical Society.

Haddon, A. C., and James Hornell. (1991). *Canoes of Oceania*. Honolulu: Bishop Museum Press.

Hezel, Francis X. S. J. (1991). *The Catholic Church in Micronesia: historical essays on the Catholic Church in the Caroline-Marshall Islands*. Chicago, IL: Loyola University Press.

Hezel, Francis X. S. J. (1995). *Strangers in their own land: a century of colonial rule in the Caroline and Marshall Islands*. Honolulu: University of Hawai'i Press.

Hezel, Francis X. S. J., and M. L. Berg, eds. (1984). *Micronesia winds of change: a book of readings on Micronesian history*. Saipan: Trust Territory of the Pacific Islands, Department of Education.

Hijikata Hisakatsu Exhibition. (1991) *Light and dream of Micronesia*. Catalog of the exhibition. November 14 through December 15. Tokyo: Setagaya Art Museum.

Hisashi, Endo, ed. (1993). Society and life in Palau. *The collective works of Hijikata Hisakatsu*. Tokyo: Sasakawa Peace Foundation.

Hockin, John Pearce (1803). *A supplement to The account of the Pelew Islands: compiled from the journals of "Panther" and "Endeavour," two vessels sent by the Honourable East India Company to those islands in the year 1790, and from the oral communications of Captain H. Wilson*. London: G. W. Nicol.

Holden, Horace A. (1836). *Narrative of the shipwreck, captivity, and sufferings of Horace Holden and Benjamin H. Nute*. Fairfield, WA: Ye Galleon Press.

Hooper, Steven. (2006). *Pacific encounters: art and divinity in Polynesia 1760–1860*. Honolulu: University of Hawai'i Press.

Hunter-Anderson, Rosalind, ed. (1990). Recent advances in Micronesian archaeology. *Micronesica: a journal of the University of Guam*. Supplement no. 2. Mangilao: University of Guam Press.

Hynd, George W. (1975). Taotaomona: a functional belief among the Chamorro. *Guam Recorder*. University of Guam, Micronesia Area Research Center. vol. 5.

Jackson, Frederick H., and Jeffery C. Marck. (1991). *Carolinean-English Dictionary*. Honolulu: University of Hawai'i Press.

Jernigan, Earle Wesley Lochukle. (1973). *A Palauan art tradition*. (Doctoral dissertation, University of Arizona).

Johannes, R. E. (1992). *Words of the lagoon: fishing and marine lore in the Palau district of Micronesia*. Los Angeles: University of California Press.

Kaeppler, Adrienne L. (1997). La vie sociale d' un masque des iles Mortlock. *Oceanie curieux, navigateurs et savants*. San Paolo: Somogy Editions D'Art.

Kaeppler, Adrienne L., Christian Kaufmann, and Douglas Newton. (1997). *Oceanic art*. New York: Harry Abrams.

Kagle, Joseph. (1976). Osiik is dead. *Glimpses of Guam*. Second Quarter. Agana, Guam: Glimpses of Guam. pp. 14–17.

Kahn, E. J. Jr. (1966). *A reporter in Micronesia*. New York: W. W. Norton and Company.

Karig, Walter. (1948). *The fortunate islands*. New York: Rinehart and Company.

Karolle, Bruce. (1988). *Atlas of Micronesia*. Honolulu: Bess Press.

Keate, George. (1788). *An account of the Pelew Islands*. London: G. Nicol.

Kitalong, Ann Hillman. (1998). *A personal Tour of Palau*. Ann Hillman Kitalong. Palau: self-published.

Kiyono, Kenji. (1942). *Nations of the Pacific Ocean and their political science*. Japan: Iwani Shotenkanko.

Klingman, Lawrence, and Gerald Green. (1950). *His Majesty O'Keefe*. New York: Charles Scribner's Sons.

Koch, Gerd. (1986). *The material culture of Kiribati*. Guy Slatter, trans. Suva: Institute of Pacific Studies, University of the South Pacific.

Kotzebue, Otto A. von. (1821). A voyage of discovery into the South Sea and Beering's Straits, for the purpose of exploring a south-east passage, undertaken in the years 1815–1818. vol. 2. London: A. and R. Spottiswoode for Hurst, Rees, Orme, and Brown.

Kotzebue, Otto A. von. (1830). A new voyage round the world in the years 1823, 1824, 1825, and 1826. vol. 1. London: Colburn and Bentley

Krämer, Augustin. (1926). Palau *Ergebnisse der Südsee-Expedition 1908–1910*. II, B, vol. 3. Hamburg: Friederichsen De Gruyter and Company.

Krämer, Augustin. (1929). Palau *Ergebnisse der Südsee-Expedition 1908–1910*. II, B, vol. 4. Hamburg: Friederichsen, De Gruyter and Company.

Krämer, Augustin. (1932). Truk *Ergebnisse der Südsee-Expedition 1908–1910*. II, B, vol. 5. Hamburg: Friederichsen, De Gruyter and Company.

Krämer, Augustin. (1935). Truk *Ergebnisse der Südsee-Expedition 1908–1910*. II, B, vol. 6. Hamburg: Friederichsen, De Gruyter and Company.

Krämer, Augustin. (1937). Zentralkarolinen, Part I (Lamotrek Gruppe, Oleai, Feis) *Ergebnisse der Südsee-Expedition 1908–1910.* G. Thilenius, ed. II, B, vol. 10. Hamburg: Friederichsen, De Gruyter and Company.

Kubary, J. S. (1885). *Ethnographische beträge zur kenntnis der Karolinischen Inselgruppe und Nachbarschaft.* Human Relations Area Files. Leiden: P. W. M. Trap.

Kubary. J. S. (1889). *Ethnographische beträge zur kenntnis des Karolinen Archipels.* Leiden: P. W. M. Trap.

LeBar, Frank M. (1964). *The material culture of Truk.* New Haven, CT: Department of Anthropology, Yale University.

Leenhardt, Maurice. (1950). *Folk art of Oceania.* New York: Tudor Publishing.

Le Geyt, Linda M. (1986). *Hand fans of Micronesia.* (Master's thesis, University of Hawai'i).

Local crafts project Kosrae community action program catalog. (1993).

Mason, Leonard. (1964). Micronesian cultures. *Encyclopedia of world art.* vol. 9. London: McGraw-Hill. pp. 915–930, plates pp. 543–548.

Matsumura, Akira. (1918). Ethnography of Micronesia: contributions to the ethnography of Micronesia. *Journal of college of science* vol. 40, art. 7. Tokyo: Imperial University of Tokyo Press.

McBean, Angus. (1964). *Handicrafts of the south seas.* Nouméa: South Pacific Commission.

McKnight, Robert E. (1964 April). *Handicrafts of the trust territory of the Pacific Islands.* Nouméa: South Pacific Bulletin.

McKnight, Robert E. (1967). Palauan storyboards. *Lore.* vol. 17, no. 3, Summer. pp. 82–88.

Meyer, Anthony J. P. (1995) *Oceanic art.* vol. 2. New York: Knickerbocker Press.

Micronesia: navigators and their culture. (1997). Catalog of the exhibition. Japan: Folk Museum of Ota City.

Mitchell, Roger. (1975). The Palauan storyboard: evolution of a folk art style. *Midwestern journal of language and folklore.* vol. 1, no. 2.

Montvel-Cohen, Marvin. (1982). *Craft and context on Yap.* (Doctoral dissertation, Southern Illinois University).

Montvel-Cohen, Marvin. (1987). *Continuity and change in the material culture of Micronesia.* Isla Center for the Arts, University of Guam.

Mulford, Judy. (1991). *Decorative Marshallese baskets.* Los Angeles: Wonder Publications.

Mulford, Judy. (2006). Handicrafts of the Marshall Islands. Majuro: Ministry of Resources and Development.

Mulford, Judy. (1980). Lava lavas of the Western Carolines. (Master's thesis, California State University, Northridge).

Nason, James D. Email to author. (February 23, 2006).

Nason, James D. Emails to author. (October 20, 2008).

Nason, James D. Emails to author. (November 24, 2009).

Nason, James, D. (1984). Tourism handicrafts and ethnic identity in Micronesia. *Annals of Tourism Research*. vol. 11. Elsevier Science, Amsterdam.

Nature's Way. (2005). www.naturesway.fm/archives/ishiwara/report. (May 17, 2005).

Nero, Karen, ed. (1992). The breadfruit tree story: mythological transformations in Palauan politics. *The Arts and Politics: Special Issue of the Journal of Pacific Studies*. 15 (4), pp. 235–260. Suva, Fiji.

Osborne, Douglas. (1966). The archaeology of the Palau Islands. *Bernice P. Bishop Museum Bulletin* 230, Honolulu: Bishop Museum.

Owen, Hera Ware. (1980). *Rechucher Charlie Gibbons: Retrospective Exhibition*. Commonwealth Arts Council of the Northern Mariana Islands. Micronesian Research Center, University of Guam.

Quarterly Report of the Administrator of Palau. (1950, January).

Pacific Worlds and Associates. (2004). "In the camps." PREL—Pacific Resources for Education and Learning. www. pacificworlds.com/cnmi/memories.

Parmentier, Richard J. (1987). *The sacred remains: myth history and polity in Belau* Chicago: University of Chicago Press.

Peattie, Mark R. (1988). *The rise and fall of the Japanese in Micronesia*, 1885–1945. Honolulu: University of Hawai'i Press.

Rainbird, Paul. (2004). *The archaeology of Micronesia*. Cambridge: Cambridge University Press.

Richard, Dorothy. (1957). The wartime military government period 1942–1945. *United States naval administration of the Trust Territory of the Pacific Islands*. vol. 1. Washington, D.C.: U.S. Government Printing Office.

Ritzenthaler, Robert E. (1954). Native money of Palau. *Publications in anthropology*. no. 1. Milwaukee: Milwaukee Public Museum.

RMI Embassy. (2008) "Embassy of the Republic of the Marshall Islands." Washington, D.C. http://www.rmiembassyus.org/index.htm.

Robinson, David, (1983). Decorative motifs of Palauan clubhouses. *Art and artists of Oceania*. Bernie Kernot and Sidney Mead, eds. Mill Valley, CA: Ethnographic Arts Publications.

Rolls, Ian. (1991). *Handicrafts of the Federated States of Micronesia*. Colonia: Government of the Federated States of Micronesia and Suva: Forum Secretariat.

Rubinstein, Donald. (1988). Learning at the loom. *Glimpses of Guam*. Third Quarter. Agana, Guam: Glimpses of Guam.

Schindlebeck, Marcus (1994). *Von kokos zu plastic. Südseekulturen im wandel*. Berlin: Museum fur Völkerkunde.

Schmitz, Carl A. (1967). *Oceanic art: myth, man, and image in the south seas*. New York: Harry N. Abrams.

Smith, Deverne Reed. (1975). The Palauan storyboards from traditional architecture to airport art. *Expedition*. Fall 1975. pp. 1–17. Philadelphia.

Someki, Atsushi. (1945). *Micronesia: Its nature and artifacts in Micronesia*. Tokyo: Shoko Shoin.

Spennemann, Dirk H. R. (1998). *Essays on the Marshallese Past*. Second edition. Albury: http://marshall.csu.edu.au/Marshalls/html/essays/es-ed-1.html.

Steager, Peter W. (1979). Where does art begin in Puluwat? *Exploring the visual art of Oceania*. Sidney Mead, ed. Honolulu: University of Hawai'i Press.

Swadling, P. (1996). *Plumes from paradise: trade cycles in South East Asia and their impact on New Guinea and nearby islands until 1920*. Bokoro: Papua New Guinea National Museum and Art Gallery.

Temengil, Jerome Esebei. (2004). *Legends of Palau*. vols. 1, 2. Koror: MoonShadow Publications.

Toomin, Phillip R., and Pauline M. Toomin. (1963). *Black robe and grass skirt*. New York: Horizon Press.

Treide, Barbara. (1997). *In den weiten des pazifik*. Museen für Völkerkunde zu Leipzig und Dresden. Weisbaden: Ludwig Reichert.

Udui, Elizabeth S. (1964). The handicraft industry in the trust territory. Occasional papers and reprints. no. 1. Saipan: Trust Territory of the Pacific Islands.

Untaman, Vincent, Vera Whitcomb, and the Ninth Grade of Yap District Intermediate School. (1956). *Yap our island*. Saipan: Yap District Department of Education, Publications Office.

Vitarelli, Margo. (1980). *The storyboard: from meeting house to money: The effects of culture contact on a Palauan art form*. (Unpublished school paper for Science 341).

Walsh, John A., and Eulaia Hurui-Walsh. (1989). Ulithian lava lava: Fabric of a culture. Island Art. *Glimpses of Guam*. Fourth Quarter. Agana, Guam: Glimpses of Guam.

Wavell, Barbara B. (1996). *The art of Micronesia*. Catalog of the exhibition. May 10 through July 7. Florida: Maitland Art Center.

Wavell, Barbara B. (2002). From sacred to souvenir: The squatting figure as a motif in Micronesian art. *Tribal Arts Magazine*. Summer 2002. San Francisco: Tribarts.

Wells, Marjorie D. (1982). *Micronesian handicraft book of the trust territory of the Pacific Islands*. New York: Carlton Press.

Yacoe, Caroline. (September 24, 2008). Marshall Islands Visitor Authority. Majuro: Media Press. www.visitmarshallislands.com/mivajapan/media.htm. (February 17, 2010).

Yanaihara, Tadao. (1940). *Pacific islands under Japanese mandate*. London: Oxford University Press.

Disclaimer
Please note that every effort has been made to identify individuals illustrated in photographs shown in this book. If we were unable to reach you, please accept our apologies. We would be glad to include your name and other information in future printings.

Belau National Museum
Ulekdubs Gift Shop
P.O. Box 666
Koror, Palau, PW 96940
Website: www.belaunationalmuseum.org
Phone: 680-488-2265
Email: ulekdubsgiftshop@belaunationalmuseum.org

Ethnic Art Institute of Micronesia (EAIM)
In the Trader's Ridge Resort
P.O. Box B
Yap, FM 96943
Website: www.tradersridge.com
Website: www.ethnicartinstitute.org
Phone: 1-877-350-1300
Email: lee@tradersridge.com

Kosrae Visitors Bureau
P.O. Box 659
Tofol, Kosrae, FM 96944
Website: www.kosrae.com
Phone: 691-370-2228

Nika Wase, Marshall Islands Weaver
P.O. Box 1156
Majuro, MH 96960
Phone: 692-455-0389
Email: libeb@ntamar.net

Reitan Ainen Kamatu (RAK) Center
P.O. Box 80
Antebuka, Tarawa
Kiribati
Phone: 686-21132
Email: rak@tskl.net.ki

Robert Reimers Enterprises, Inc.
Handicrafts of the Marshall Islands
Attention: Jessica Reimers
P.O. Box 1
Majuro, MH 96960
Website: www.rreinc.com/retail.html
Phone: 692-625-3250
Email: rreadmin@ntamar.net

Teitoiningaina Women's Centre
P.O. Box 79
Bairiki, Tarawa
Kiribati
Phone: 686-21038
Email: teitoiningaina@tskl.net.ki

Yap Art Studio and Gallery
Lonnie Fread, Contact
P.O. Box 949
Yap, FM 96943
Website: www.yapartstudioandgallery.com
Phone: 691-350-4180
Email: yapeseart@mail.fm

WEBSITE LINKS

Bazaar Planet
www.bazaarplanet.com

Friends of Tobi Island
tobi.gmu.edu

Micronesian Seminar
www.micsem.org

Pacific Arts Association
pacificarts.org

Pacific Worlds
www.pacificworlds.com

"From Sacred to Souvenir: The Squatting Figure as a Motif in Micronesian Art"
by Barbara B. Wavell
www.tribalarts.com/feature/index.html

Handicrafts of the Marshall Islands by Judy Mulford
www.visitmarshallislands.com/pdf/Handicraftbooklet.pdf

Marshallese Handicrafts by Dirk Spennemann
micronesia.csu.edu.au/Marshalls/html/Handicraft/Handicraft.html

SEARCHABLE DATABASES

Bishop Museum
Honolulu, HI
www.bishopmuseum.org

Burke Museum of Natural History and Culture
Seattle, WA
www.washington.edu/burkemuseum/collections

Peabody Museum of Archaeology and Ethnology
Harvard, MA
www.peabody.harvard.edu

Smithsonian Institution
Washington, D.C.
www.si.edu

Spurlock Museum, University of Illinois
Urbana-Champaign, IL
www.spurlock.uiuc.edu

FIGURE 137

FRONT COVER AND FACING PAGE: See Figure 23.

FIGURE 1: *Cigarette box, Republic of Palau, Unknown Carver*
Wood, pigments, nails, 10" high, 1940s–1950s
This representation of a Palauan *bai* is decorated in what Jernigan calls "new style" based on the *dilukai* figure on the front. The roof can be lifted, the inside filled with filterless cigarettes then replaced. Once it is lifted again, one cigarette rolls onto hollowed platform, which remains fixed in the top of the roof. The construction of this cigarette box was probably taught to Palauans during the Japanese period. Decorated boxes utilizing the same principle are found in China, India, and Japan. The *bai* or men's house represents a cultural symbol converted to a use appealing to visitors, who were often smokers during the 1940s and 1950s. Thus, this item is an example of the process of familiarization.

FIGURE 2: *Male and Female Figure Pair, Kuttu, Mortlock Islands, Chuuk State, FSM, Unknown Carvers*
Wood, pigments, 11⅜" and 9⅞," 1946, and (central statue) 15," 1950s
The matched figure pair was purchased by a Navy officer on the isle of Chuuk immediately after WWII. The pair has large heads, smaller bodies, and, from the side, appears to be slanting backwards. They were covered with a kind of dark varnish that obscured the color of their skirt and loincloth, some of which has been removed. The central figure was mounted on a stand by a previous owner. It lacks the characteristic ear spools of the figure pair and epitomizes the sumo-like style in which these statues were often carved through the early 1960s.

FIGURE 3: *Storyboard: The Breadfruit Tree, Negotiating for Peace, Men Carrying Money, Republic of Palau, Ngiraibuuch*
Wood, commercial paints, 30" x 8," 24" x 7," and 14" x 6," 1950s early 1960s
The first board may represent the seventh time that the *Ibedul* (leader of Koror in Palau) came to conquer Airai (another municipality), and a female chief offered her own money to settle the conflict. The second storyboard depicts the Breadfruit Tree Story, which is a popular and iconic story having cultural and political significance for the nation of Palau. The story tells of an old woman who could not feed herself. A god gave her a magic tree, and, when she cut off a branch, fish came pouring through. When the villagers found out, they became jealous and cut the tree down, causing the island to sink (Wavell 1996:17). This was one of two painted boards, which were the first to be acquired during the 1980s. The third board depicts Yapese carrying a heavy wheel of stone money. These three richly detailed boards with careful layouts and clamshell boarders are very characteristic of the early work of Ngiraibuuch.

FIGURE 4: *Weather Charm , Ifaluk, Yap State, FSM, Unknown Carver*
Weather Charm in janus form, approx 12," wood and mother of pearl with stingray, wood, and dog bone spines, 2004
Weather charms were traditionally held up in four directions before a voyage to ensure good winds, a safe journey, and protection from evil influences. This charm has coconut fronds tied around it as did sacred statues in the 1800s. This carving was donated to the Outer Islands Cultural Program in 2004 to raise money for island schools and is missing the lime, which would have secured stingray spines at the base of the statue. This example had one broken stingray spine, one dog bone spine, and two carved wood spines. To save stingrays, replicas today are made with wooden spines. Based on the variety of broken spines on this example, it may have experienced a period of "use." However, most truly authentic weather charms date no later than the 1950s or 1960s when traditional belief systems were still very much intact. They often had painted on eyes, beards, and other features, rather than the inlaid eyes seen in this example, and their hands blended into the base of the statue, unlike this example. This beautifully carved statue was probably produced by a master carver who also carved squatting figures, hence the inlaid eyes.

FIGURE 5: *Photograph*
This photograph of the Palauan wood carver, Osiik, carving a statue using his adze was taken in 1966 by Norden Cheatham and has been made available for this publication through the generosity of the Micronesian Seminar.

FIGURE 6: *Male and Female Figure Pair, Republic of Palau, Osiik*
Wood, natural fibers, cowry shells, mother of pearl inlay, 23" each, early 1950s
These figures, which have "Osiik" carved across their base, were obtained from the Volkner estate. Volkner was in Yap in the late 1940s with the air force and was stationed in Guam for six years through the early 1950s. These figures are interesting since they have natural fiber skirts and necklaces, which appear similar to those which were made in the Marshall Islands at the time.

FIGURE 7: *Photograph*
This photograph shows an elderly man making a traditional stick navigation chart. It looks like a *mattang*, which is used to teach patterns of swells usually around a particular island. This photo was taken by Giff Johnson around 1980 and was provided courtesy of the Micronesian Seminar.

FIGURE 8: *Navigation Chart, Republic of the Marshall Islands, Unknown Craftsman*
Sticks, coconut fiber twine, shells, 29¼" x 26½," 1950s
This stick chart from the Hogan estate is called a *rebbelib* since it illustrates not only patterns of currents but the location of islands in a group of islands. It came from the collection of John Hamilton Hogan, who worked for NBC and helped hook up the sound for FDR's fireside chats. During WWII, he joined the navy ending the war as a Commander and then worked for the navy as a civil servant in Guam from the early 1950s through 1971, during which time he accumulated a large number of handicrafts.

FIGURE 9: *Photograph*
This photograph, taken in Pohnpei around 1970, depicts a woman weaving a large, decorative wall mat using teneriffe and shells. From the collection of the College of Micronesia, this photograph was made available courtesy of the Micronesian Seminar.

FIGURE 10: *Basket, Republic of the Marshall Islands, Unknown Weaver*
Coconut palm, pandanus, commercial dyes, gold ringer cowries, 16½" square, 1990s
This Republic of the Marshall Islands wall mat cleverly incorporates the national flag into the center of a design edged with cowries and finished off with decorative corners of teneriffe. Mats similar to this and the one shown in Figure 9 are made in Kosrae, Pohnpei and the Marshall Islands.

FIGURE 11: *Folding Bookrack, Republic of Palau, Unknown Carver*
Wood, mother of pearl inlay, 7½"x 14," 1950s–1960s
Palauans were probably taught to make these folding bookracks in carpentry schools during the Japanese period. The carvings are based on traditional Palauan post figures, but a similar design of folding bookrack is found throughout Europe and Asia.

FIGURES 12 AND 13: *Hand fans, Republic of the Marshall Islands, Unknown Weavers*
Kimej over wooden handle, both 12½" long with handle, early 1940s, 1960s
Although often referred to as "Kosrae" fans based on Marjorie Wells description (Well 1982:76, 108), Linda La Geyt's master's thesis makes it clear that this style of fan was also made extensively in the Marshall Islands, and it is likely to have originated there. Figure 12, which was labeled as having come from Lae in the Marshalls, has a tightly woven complex handle design and a more complex face design than Figure 13. The two fans are a good example of the process of simplification. But finely made fans continued to be woven well into the late twentieth century, so Figure 13 may also be the work of a novice fan maker.

FIGURE 14: *Squatting Figure, Republic of Palau, Unknown Carver*
Wood, red paint, mother of pearl, 14" tall and 7" wide, 1960s
This large monkey woman has a massive tray-like headpiece, which is decorated with the Palauan clamshell motif—symbolic of money and used as a border on storyboards. This unusual statue was probably carved by a Tobi carver on Palau or possibly a Palauan storyboard carver, since it includes Palauan motifs.

FIGURE 15: *Photograph*
A group of female students are dancing in celebration at the High School graduation of the class of 1965 on Yap. Photo was taken by Albert Miller who worked on the construction of the navy signal relay station in 1965.

FIGURE 16: *Photograph*
A Yapese men's house or *falu* with pieces of stone money leaning against it can be seen through the hole in a large piece of stone money, providing a window into the distinctive traditional nature of Yap culture. This photograph was provided by Russ and Marilyn Aldridge, who were SDA missionaries and teachers in Palau during the 1960s.

FIGURE 17: *Male and Female Figure Pair, Republic of Palau, Osiik*
Dort wood, mother of pearl, twine, and natural fibers, 20" tall and 4½," wide and mounted to a 22" long board, 1950s–1971
These figures, from the estate of John Hogan, have been carved individually and can be slotted into a board that forms the base of the figure pair. (See Figure 8.) The statues are tentatively attributed to Osiik, based on a photograph of another pair also said to be by Osiik with similar, distinctive, protruding ears.

FIGURE 18: *Kuttu Figure, Kuttu, Mortlock Islands, Chuuk State, FSM*
Wood, pigments, 15," 1950s
This statue is described in detail in Figure 2.

FIGURE 19: *Men Twisting Sakau, Pohnpei State, FSM, Depit Gamson*
Wood, 14½" long x 11" high, 1960s
Sakau is the root material that is processed to produce *kava*, and, in this style of genre scene unique to Pohnpei, two men are shown twisting the plant material to produce the potent drink. At least two different carvers have been documented to carve this style of figure. Deruit Marume won first place in 1970 in the second annual Micronesian Arts Festival for a pair in a similar pose but with uniquely different facial features. The Peabody Essex museum also has a nearly identical example said to be carved by Depit Gamson. This example was originally acquired by Joe Kagle in the 1960s.

FIGURE 20: *Photograph*
Here the author poses with stone money in Yap in June of 2004. This photograph gives some idea of the large size of some of these wheels of stone. This photograph belongs to the author.

FIGURE 21: *Photograph*
This photo, taken in Yap in the summer of 2004, shows two men rebuilding the stone platform surrounding a men's house or *falu* after the destruction wrought by an April typhoon. These club houses are proudly maintained and are still an important part of Yapese life. This photograph belongs to the author.

FIGURE 22: *Men Carrying Stone Money, Yap State, FSM, Gilfalan*
Breadfruit wood, black paint, red cloth, natural fibers, crystallized calcite, 12½" tall, 1960s
One characteristic of Gilfalan's carvings is the thick base, which is left as a natural log with bark attached. This amazing well proportioned carving is carved from a single piece of wood and depicts a classic Yapese scene, also often seen on Palauan storyboards, of men carrying stone money. This statue came from the estate of a man who may have been associated with the U.S. press corps during and immediately after WWII.

FIGURE 23: *Male and Female Figure Pair in Traditional Dress, Ngulu Island, Yap State, FSM, Judge Fanechoor*
Breadfruit fibers, black paint, red cloth, 20¼" and 19½," 1930s–1940s
These statues were collected by a female travel agent who traveled throughout Asia and the Pacific. Bought in a curio shop in the Far East, these statues were likely produced during the Japanese period.

FIGURE 24: *Three Figures in Traditional Dress, Ulithi, Yap State, FSM, Guar*
Breadfruit wood, red and black paint, blue and red trade cloth, natural fibers, chicken feathers 12½," 15," and 16," late 1950s, early 1960s
This style of figure is very well known, and examples are found in a number of museums (see text).

FIGURE 25: *Photograph*
This photograph of Guar, carving a statue while a young boy looks on, was taken in 1951 by Father William Walter, a Jesuit priest on Ulithi, and has been made available for publication courtesy of the Micronesian Seminar.

FIGURE 26: *Male and Female Figure Pair, Makei Village, Yap State, FSM, Rudolf Ken*
Wood, natural fibers, black ink, 18" and 20" tall, 2005 and 2007
These statues, carved by the deaf carver Rudolf Ken, are dressed in traditional dress and holding authentically woven bags or *waey*, which are used to store betel nut and other personal items. The beautiful, striped, colored skirt worn by the woman is of a style used in dance skirts today. One main difference between this contemporary statue and those from the 1950s is that the hair, beard, nipples, and other features are not painted in, and Ken's statues appear to have characteristically foreshortened arms. These statues were obtained through the Yap Art Studio and Gallery.

FIGURE 27: *Tapuanu Masks, Mortlock Islands, Chuuk State, FSM, Unknown Artist*
Breadfruit wood, black and white pigments, 14" and 14½," 1950s
These small masks, similar to those that would have been used to ornament gable ends rather than being worn, came from the Hogan estate. (See Figure 8.)

FIGURE 28: *Male and Female Figure Pair, Kuttu Island, Mortlock Islands, Chuuk State, FSM, Unknown Artist*
Wood, natural pigments, 15" and 16", 1900s–1930s
This very early Kuttu figure pair was said to have been obtained from European dealers for a private New England collection. The figures are shown wearing the Mortlock mask and may have been carved by men belonging to a secret society associated with the cult of the masks. The statues were then purchased by Taylor Dale and subsequently sold via Tribalmania. They now reside in a private collection. This photograph is courtesy of Tribalmania.

FIGURE 29: *Male and Female Figure Pair, Kuttu Island, Mortlock Islands, Chuuk State, FSM, Unknown Artist*
Breadfruit wood, black and red pigments, both 11" tall, 1950s
These figures with ear spools were collected by Frankie Teel Mayo between 1950 and 1957 when she was acting postmistress on Chuuk. Donated by her son Ronald Mayo, they are beautiful examples of the clean, almost geometric lines characteristic of this style.

FIGURE 30: *Back to Back Figures, Kuttu Island, Mortlocks Islands, Chuuk State, FSM, Unknown Artist*
Breadfruit wood, black and red pigments, 8½" tall x 6½" wide, 1950s
The two figures with ear spools are posed with their heads back to back in a *janus* motif otherwise only seen in weather charms. This pose may represent vigilance—looking both ways to spot the coming storm. Extremely similar in style to the figures collected by Frankie Teel Mayo above, they were likely made by the same carver.

FIGURE 31: *Photograph*
By 1951, when this photo was taken, only elderly people on Chuuk still had the stretched out earlobes, which once accommodated large ear spools and other heavy ornaments. This photo, taken by Frankie Teel Mayo, has been provided courtesy of Ron Mayo.

FIGURE 32: *Mother and Child, Kuttu Island, Mortlock Islands, Chuuk State, FSM, Unknown Artist*
Breadfruit wood, 13" high, 1950s
Though islanders are generally very careful to keep their thighs covered, surprisingly, this female figure's crudely carved and bare legs are exposed. She holds a tiny child as if she has recently given birth. This figure can be identified as a Kuttu carving from its ear spools and stylized lines.

FIGURE 33: *Standing Figures, Chuuk State, FSM, Unknown Artists*
Wood colored with shoe polish, 13½," 15½," 15," and 18," 1980s–1990s
This group of figures represents a style still being produced today. Common poses include holding spears, fish nets, or, in one case, a giant fish.

FIGURE 34: *Man with Pounder, Chuuk State, FSM, Unknown Carver*
Wood, 13½," 1970s–1980s
This genre figure depicts a Chuukese man pounding breadfruit. Surplus breadfruit can be pounded and stored in pits where it is allowed to ferment as a source of food once the breadfruit season is over. This is a very well done example of a modern sculptural style, which developed in the 1960s. Similar carvings are being produced today. From the estate of Bernadette Wherly, this carving was a gift from Father Fran Hezel and the Micronesian Seminar.

FIGURE 35: *Male and Female Figure Pair, Republic of Palau, Heinrich Dort wood, 20" tall, 1960s*

Today all carved statues, such this male and female pair, are called *dilukai* in Palau. However, they bear little resemblance to the famous female figure whose legs were once spread over the entrance of the *bai*. There are many versions of the *dilukai* story and its meaning has been disputed. Later versions, perhaps influenced by Christian missionaries, sometimes view the revealing pose of the *dilukai* as punishment for some kind of immoral behavior.

FIGURE 36: *Photograph*

Georg Fritz was a district officer in Saipan from 1899 to 1907. This photograph appears to depict Palauan women holding and possibly dancing with statues on their heads. This photo may have been taken on Saipan of Palauans who were exiled there due to religious and political protests. This photograph was taken by Georg Fritz in 1905 and is made available for publication courtesy of the Micronesian Area Research Center (MARC).

FIGURE 37: *Male and Female Figure Pair, Republic of Palau, Unknown Carver Heavy wood (possibly dort), inlaid eyes, 12" high, 1960s*

This beautifully done figure pair shows the female in a classic pose, with a basket over her head, while the male is fully armed with a club and spear. With Trust Territory price tags attached, these statues were probably made by the same carver who produced a pair of carvings documented in the Trust Territory Archives (3383.02 TTFF).

FIGURE 38: *Woman at First Child Ceremony, Republic of Palau, Ling Inabo, Tebang Studio Wood, colored pigments, woven flower, 13¾" tall, 1999*

In 2004, when this statue was purchased, Ling Inabo, a prominent contemporary storyboard artist, advised that this was the last figural sculpture he would produce, since it is one carving task he cannot turn over to his apprentices. The statue depicts a woman taking part in the First Child Ceremony. Wearing traditional money around her neck, she has been kept in a special hut and bathed in hot water mixed with medicinal leaves. Even today, women wear fiber skirts (often now using cotton thread) and assume this classic pose, holding a flower in one hand.

FIGURE 39: *Male and Female Figure Pair, Sonsorol, Republic of Palau, Lee Pedro Breadfruit wood, mother of pearl, pigments, 12½" tall, 2004*

This male/female pair of statues was carved by Lee Pedro for the Ninth Festival of Pacific Arts in 2004. These beautifully proportioned statues were purchased in the Sonsorol booth on the last day of the festival. Lee Pedro has been carving such statues pairs since the early 1990s. Other examples of his work can be seen in the Etpison museum and the Palau Hotel in Koror, Palau, but with hair that has been inked in. Perhaps the artist did not have time on this pair. The detailed tattoo patterns on both male and female figures evoke the cultural connections between southwest islands, such as Sonsorol, and out islands surrounding Yap.

FIGURE 40: *Chip carved Figure Group, Saipan, CNMI, Unknown Artists Wood, colored pigments, squatting figures in foreground are all approximately 6" high, 1940s, early 1950s, standing figures are 9¾," 12," and 12½," late 1940s, early 50s*

These statues are all chip carved, revealing individual carving marks. Some have skirts in traditional Carolinian colors (red and green) and have garlands of flowers in their hair. These statues, sold as souvenirs to American servicemen shortly after WWII, may have been carved in Camp Susupe, a prisoner internment camp on Saipan.

FIGURE 41: *Female Figure, Saipan, CNMI, Caroline Islander on Saipan*
Wood, 9¾" tall, late 1940s
This figure, the first of this style encountered by the author, epitomizes a genre figure, which is repeated time and again—a standing woman wearing a grass skirt and holding a bowl of fruit.

FIGURE 42: *Female Figure, Saipan, CMNI, Caroline Islander on Saipan*
Wood 9¼" tall, late 1940s
This crudely chip-carved statue was described as having come from the estate of a retired USMC Sergeant. This example is the proverbial "smoking gun," which identifies all these figures since she is mounted a large block of wood on which the words "Saipan" are incised.

FIGURE 43: *Male Figure, Saipan, CMNI, Caroline Islander on Saipan*
Wood, fiber, 13," late 1940s
This chip-carved figure with a fiber loincloth carries a small stick in his hand. He reinforces the cohesive style already established by other Saipan figures seen here.

FIGURE 44: *Bowl with Figures, Saipan, CMNI, Caroline Islands Carver on Saipan*
Carved figures and coconut bowl mounted on mangrove wood, 6" x 4½" wide, mid-1940s
This bowl is another example of a chip-carved tradition that developed in Saipan and stopped being produced shortly after WWII. Similar figures can be seen in photos of handicraft exhibits taken at the time.

FIGURE 45: *Mannguchig Outrigger Canoe, Saipan, CMNI, Yap Islander on Saipan?*
Wood, pigments, bamboo slats, 17" x 11," 1945
This outrigger was said to have been brought back from Saipan by a serviceman in 1945. Probably made by Caroline Islanders who came from Yap during the Japanese period and were held in internment camps immediately after the war, the canoe depicts a traditional style of Yapese outrigger called a *mannguchig*. This Yapese style of canoe known for its distinctive moveable canoe prow ornaments is no longer being made today on Yap, not even in model form. On the canoe are two carved figures—a man is holding a piece of Yapese money, while a woman appears to be holding a fish trap or a bail of some kind. This canoe was in terrible shape and missing a boom and many connecting sticks. It was restored over a period of six months by the author's father-in-law Harry Lamberty.

FIGURE 46: *Photograph*
This photograph shows sailors from the USS *Orca* bartering for handicrafts, Ngatik, Pohnpei, 1946. Immediately after WWII, a large population of servicemen sought souvenirs of their war experience, sometimes bartering for them with cigarettes. This photograph from the Naval Historic Society was made available for publication courtesy of the Micronesian Seminar.

FIGURE 47: *Club, Saipan, CMNI*
This club, incised "Saipan 1946," was awarded to an officer who was present when native Carolinians were liberated from Camp Susupe after WWII. It has a traditional Chuukese look, which is not surprising since islanders from Chuuk State have migrated to Saipan in the centuries after the Spanish occupation.

FIGURE 48: *Squatting Figure, Ulithi Island, Yap State, FSM, Unknown Artist*
Wood, mother of pearl, 7" tall and 4" wide, 1960s
This figure epitomizes a Ulithi style squatting figure with its huge angular eyes and blocky form.

FIGURE 49: *Squatting Figure, Satawan, Mortlock Islands, Chuuk State, FSM, Unknown Artist*
Wood, dark pigment (on brows), 10½" tall, 1930s–1940s
A very similar carving, shown in Adrienne Kaeppler's *Oceanic Art* (1997:435), was acquisitioned by the Smithsonian in 1959 and was said to have been collected in Satawan in the Mortlocks. Another almost identical statue was recently acquired by the Metropolitan. These figures have more distinctive eyebrows than "Tobi" style squatting figures from other areas. The eyebrows are slightly evocative of Mortlock masks. There was a Japanese airbase on Satawan, so whether squatting figures were native to this culture area or simply developed to sell to visitors during the Japanese period whence they were exported to the Japanese capital in Palau is unclear. Certainly the Mortlocks have their own well documented *tapuanu* masks and figures.

FIGURES 50 AND 51: *Double Squatting Figure, Tobi, Republic of Palau, Unknown Artist*
Wood, mother of pearl, 5¼," 1930s–1940s
This figure is unique since it has the outline of a classic "monkeyman," as depicted in Kenji Kiyono's book *Nations of the Pacific Ocean and their Political Science.* (Kiyono's graphic is shown as part of Figure 51.) Further, the genitals are detailed, another indication that this carving may date to the Japanese period. It comes from the collection of Hera Ware Owen.

FIGURE 52: *Standing and Squatting Monkeymen Figures, Tobi, Republic of Palau, Patricio Tahimaremaho*
Wood, mother of pearl, both 9½," smaller figure 4," 1960s
These standing "monkeymen" figures have Trust Territory labels and round staring eyes- a compelling variation also found in Tobi style squatting figures such as the smaller "baby."

FIGURE 53: *Squatting Figure Pair, Tobi, Republic of Palau, Unknown Carver*
Wood, mother of pearl, 4" and 5½," 1930s–1950s
These statues were collected by the famous Smithsonian botanist Frederick Raymond Fosberg who traveled extensively in Micronesia collecting plant samples from the 1930s through the 1950s. He was one of few Westerners allowed into Micronesia during the Japanese period, and these early style figures were likely collected then. Both have their genitalia detailed, a practice that abandoned early in the Trust Territory period. These figures evoke Mortlock style figures with their heavy brows and blocky knees and shoulders.

FIGURE 54: *Dilukai Style Squatting Figures, Tobi, Republic of Palau, Unknown Artist*
Wood, mother of pearl, 6½," 6½," 7," and 7½," 1930s–1940s
Hera Ware Owen reported that this style of monkeyman was still being sold in handicraft shops in Guam when she came to Palau in 1949. This style is also depicted in Atsushi Someki's book *Micronesia: Its Nature and Artifacts*, published during the Japanese period.

FIGURE 55: *Squatting Figure, Ngulu, Yap State, FSM, Unknown Carver*
Wood, mother of pearl, pigment, 6¼" tall, 1950s
This squatting figure is a clear example of a Ngulu "frogman," with painted eyebrows, whose fat belly and breasts seem to imply a fertility motif. A similar statue is illustrated in Eugenie Clark's book *Lady with a Spear* (Clark 1951:157).

FIGURE 56: *Batman Ears Squatting Figure Pair, Tobi, Republic of Palau, Patricio Tahimaremaho*
Wood, mother of pearl, 6," 6¾," mid-1960s
These statues, documented as being produced by Tahimaremaho by Dr. Peter Black, are good examples of the kinds of innovations in style that are continually being developed by individual carvers.

FIGURE 57: *Squatting Figure, Ulithi, Yap State, FSM, Unknown Carver*
Wood, mother of pearl, 20" tall, late 1950s early 1960s
This photo depicts a very large, Ulithi-style monkeyman. Not only is it nearly two-feet tall but it is over eight-and-a-half inches wide. A statue of this unusual size with its huge eyes seems to project an eerie, mystical power.

FIGURE 58: *Squatting Figure Pair, Tobi, Republic of Palau, Basilios*
Wood, mother of pearl inlay, 6" and 4¼" tall, 1950s, 1960s
These "monkeymen" figures are classic "Tobi" style and may have been carved by Basilios, a carver from Tobi who immigrated to Palau and produced many statues. The taller of the two statues was the first monkeyman the author encountered.

FIGURE 59: *Storyboard: Bai Scene, Republic of Palau, Sbal*
Wood, pigment, 17¾" x 14¼," November 1951
This vertically oriented board depicting a Palauan *bai* or clubhouse was a very popular early board and many similar boards were produced during the 1950s.

FIGURE 60: *Photograph*
The Belau Museum *bai* is shown in the process of construction in 1969. The incised stories and symbols are clearly visible against the sky, since beams are customarily installed before the thatched roof is applied. This photograph is courtesy of Hera Ware Owen.

FIGURE 61: *Photograph*
The Belau Museum *bai* was completed and dedicated in 1969, but, unfortunately, it was destroyed by arson in 1979. There is now a new *bai* on the Belau Museum grounds. Here the beams across the front of the *bai* as well as those inside the structure are decorated with symbols and stories which are also often applied to that popular art form—the storyboard. This photograph is courtesy of Hera Ware Owen.

FIGURE 62: *Storyboard: Headhunting Scene, Republic of Palau, Unknown Carver*
Wood, colored pigments, 19½" x 4," late 1930s, early 1940s
This very early storyboard comes from the Japanese period and was collected as war booty by Second Lt. Gilbert Small, Jr. at Guadalcanal. He was a forward observer whose job it was to sight Japanese positions. He took this board from the belongings of a dead Japanese soldier. The soldier had probably purchased it while in Palau, the Japanese administrative center for the region. It appears to depict a historic Palauan battle in which many heads have been taken and attached to a skull rack. The back has a Japanese inscription as well as a circular stamp stating "passed by the naval censors."

FIGURE 63: *Storyboard: Breadfruit Tree Story, Republic of Palau, Osiik*
Wood, pigments, 46½" x 11" wide, 1950s
This board, in the form of a lump headed parrot fish, is a rare example of a painted storyboard by Osiik. Better known for his unpainted boards, this board utilizes his distinctive style of figures and speech scrolls. This is a lively version of the Breadfruit Tree Story—an important story that has become a symbol of Palau and that decorates many important buildings in Palau today. (See Figure 3 for story.) Some similar boards can be seen in Wells (1982:97).

FIGURE 64: *Storyboard: Guap and the First Childbirth Story, Republic of Palau, Linus Ngiraibuuch*
Wood, paint, 29½" x 9," 2004
This board was carved by Linus Ngiraibuuch who is the son of Ngiraibuuch Skedong, a famous early carver. Linus is one of the few carvers who still produce painted storyboards on the island, though he is apparently not as reliably prolific as his father was. He has been strongly influenced by early story images on *bai* recorded by Augustin Krämer during the South Sea Expedition 1908–1910. The blue on this board represents a popular color for houses and is also present in the Palauan flag, while the wavy chipped background evokes the corrugated iron that is used for roofing and walls in some homes. The outline of a *toluk* or piece of traditional women's money acts as a frame for two different stories, each depicted in a single scene. One is the First Childbirth story, in which a spider god teaches humans that they do not have to cut out babies with a knife. The other story is that of the giant named Guap, whose body explodes and forms the islands of Palau. (See Figure 65 below.)

FIGURE 65: *Storyboard: Story of Guap, Republic of Palau, Tebang (Ling Inabo)*
Wood, pigments, 12" x 6¾," July 12, 2004
Tebang is known for making extremely large boards and tables. This small example illustrates the story of the giant named Guap who ate and ate until the people became afraid and could no longer feed him. Then, they tied him down and set fire to him. He exploded, and pieces of his body formed the islands of Palau. This board, completed by one of Ling Inabo's apprentices, uses Tebang's characteristic style. The hair style and thick stylized thighs are reminiscent of Osiik, while the process of tinting the board with pigments was pioneered by Bernardino. Different influences collide together to form a fresh distinctive style that makes Tebang one of the most sought after carvers on the island.

FIGURE 66: *Storyboard: Breadfruit Tree Story, Republic of Palau, Unknown Carver*
Wood, 30" x 11," late 1980s–1990s
This board, shaped like a lump headed parrot fish is yet another representation of the popular Breadfruit Tree Story. It has many characteristics of modern boards including the use of a fish or turtle shape as well as the incorporation of separate scenes into the head and tail of the fish. This board is representative of the modern, "prison style" of unpainted board and may, in fact, have been carved by an inmate.

FIGURE 67: *Storyboard: Yapese Money Scene, Republic of Palau, Bernardino Rdulaol*
Wood, pigments, 32" x 12," 1960s
This medium sized irregular board is signed by Bernardino and illustrates the Yapese money story. It is a classic example of Bernardino's style—utilizing pigments for shading and the principals of depth perspective including the perspective *bai*. It was obtained from the Hogan estate.

FIGURE 68: *Storyboards: Egg Laying Cycle of the Turtle, Palauan Money, and Battle Scene, Republic of Palau, Ngiraibuuch and Unknown Carvers*
Wood, pigments, 24" x 11," 1970s, 36" x 5¾," 37½" x 6¼," 24" x 6½," 1940s–1950s
The first board shown here illustrates the egg laying cycle of the turtle. Two lovers meet on a remote island, and the girl's skirt becomes ensnared by an egg laying turtle. Thirty days later at the full moon, the lovers return and see the same turtle carrying the girls skirt returning to lay another clutch of eggs, establishing that egg laying occurs at thirty day intervals. This modern story by Ngiraibuuch uses a gouged border, which may symbolize the vine twig of Ngerot, the island where bead money was traditionally discovered. It also illustrates the perspective *bai*. The first early new style board below depicts the same story, this one in a series of separate scenes from left to right with the side view of the *bai*. The next board likely tells another version of the story of Palauan money, while the final board depicts a war party. The three "new style" boards can be identified by the amount of empty space surrounding the incised design, the frantically gesticulating figures, which are sometimes arranged above each other, and the plain, zigzag border. The final board in this group comes from the collection of Hera Ware Owen.

FIGURE 69: *Storyboard: The Dugong Maiden, Republic of Palau, Richard Silmai*
Wood, pigments, 10¾" x 15¾," January 2001
In one of his earliest boards, Richard Silmai has used dark ink to highlight the tail of a dugong maiden, the roof of the *bai* and the fruit of the keam tree, which was the cause of the problem presented in this story. Once, a young girl loved keam fruit, but, because she had just had a baby, she was forbidden to eat it. Just as she gave in to temptation, her mother saw her eating, and so she ran out to the water. As she swam, she turned into a dugong, an endangered species in Palau. Her tiny baby cried for her, but she never returned. This is the origin of a young mother being paid a bead of money otherwise called a *kluk* with the birth of a child. Richard Silmai's unique, deeply carved, shaded style is based on the early storyboard images recorded by Krämer. Along with a friend, Silmai also carves satirical carvings with double messages. For example, a carving of large feet, large hands, and a dollar sign symbolizes Palau's dependence on the U.S.

FIGURE 70: *Photograph*
Hera Ware Owen, acting Director of the Belau National Museum from 1951 to 1978, was instrumental in promoting Charles Gibbons. In this photograph, taken in 1979, Hera Ware Owen discusses with Charles Gibbons a photograph of a *bai* taken during the German period. Photograph was provided courtesy of Hera Ware Owen.

FIGURE 71: *Illustration*
This watercolor (8½" x 6") of men performing a war dance before a *bai* was painted by the famous folk artist Charles Gibbons. It was published in the catalog for Gibbon's Retrospective Exhibition held in CNMI in 1980 (#17).

FIGURE 72: *Graphic*
This watercolor by Tommy Tamangmed depicts western "tall ships" trading with the Yapese in early times, illustrating the theme of this book.

FIGURE 73: *Photograph*
Taken in October of 1969, the carver Ngirangsil is carving an *ongal* or fish dish with his adze in the Belau National Museum *bai*. Note that the traditionally hafted adze has a metal blade. Palauans began to substitute metal blades in their adzes as soon as they became available, early in the twentieth century. This photograph is courtesy of Hera Ware Owen.

FIGURE 74: *Tackle box, Puluwat, Yap District, FSM, Unknown Carver*
Wood, natural fiber, 7½" long, 1965
According to Peter Steager in "Where Does Art Begin in Puluwat" the average length of this style of tackle box is more like fifteen inches, but this one could still hold some betel nut chew and float like a boat.

FIGURE 75: *Four Bowls*
These four bowls are all from Palau and include two *ongal* or fish dishes in the middle left (15½" x 9" x 3") and on the right (18½" x 8½"), a large taro bowl (19½" x 6") on a low pedestal in the back, and a small bowl (10"x 9"x 4") in the foreground. Most of these bowls were originally purchased by Hera Ware Owen at the annual Palauan craft fairs, which started in 1952 and continued for fifteen years. Several of the larger bowls were lent by Hera for the feast celebrating the investiture of the *Ibedul* (Chief) of Koror around 1975.

FIGURE 76: *Bird-Shaped Bowl, Satawal, Yap State, FSM, Unknown Carver*
Breadfruit wood, fiber cord, palm flower cover, 17" long, 2004
This bird-shaped bowl, possibly in the shape of a frigate bird, is used to hold tattoo ink. It comes with a piece of the sheath enclosing a palm flower, which has loose fibers and can be used as a brush. It was obtained in 2004 through the Outer Island Culture Program. The bird has been tied at neck and tail with handmade twine so that it can be hung from the ceiling. Although it is an authentically made object, this example has not been used.

FIGURE 77: *Omail or Coconut Palm Wine Containers (left to right) Melekeok, Republic of Palau; Yap State, FSM; Sonsorol, Republic of Palau; and Angaur, Republic of Palau, Unknown Craftsmen*
Coconuts, coconut fiber twine, 4" to 6" in diameter, 2004
These containers, used for carrying water or palm wine, are traditionally looped onto a stick so they can then be carried over the shoulder.

FIGURE 78: *Photograph*
This photograph, taken by Dr. Donald Rubinstein on Fais in 1976, shows boys playing with sailing vessels. Their names, from left to right, include Isaac Ubud, Santiago Mangemog, Alfonso Hadagobey, Thomas Mangirchog, and Tino Ragmangu. Thanks to Dr. Rubinstein for allowing us to use this photograph.

FIGURE 79: *Outrigger Canoe, Satawal or Ifaluk Atoll, Yap State, FSM, Unknown Craftsman*
Breadfruit wood, fiber twine, black and yellow pigment, 24" long, October 28, 1953
This canoe was collected by Ted Bayer, a zoologist who was part of the expedition to Ifaluk described in Marston Bates's and Donald Abbott's *Coral Island: Portrait of an Atoll* from September 12 to November 9, 1953. A label accompanying the outrigger provided the date and the word "Mangyan," which may be the carver's name.

FIGURE 80: *Fish Trap, Satawal Atoll, Yap State, FSM, Unknown Craftsman*
Wood, twine, 20" x 10," 2004
This model fish trap was obtained on Yap through the Outer Islands Culture Program. Full sized it would take four men to carry it. It would have been placed at the outlet where a lagoon empties into the sea and fish would become trapped as the tide went out.

FIGURE 81: *Outrigger Canoe Model, Yap State, FSM, Unknown Maker*
Wood, paint, coconut fiber, 15" long x 11" wide, 1960s
This style of outrigger canoe called a *powpow*, has a bifurcated prow and is brightly painted in red, white, and black. *Powpows*, used for travel and fishing, are still being used today.

FIGURE 82: *Fish Hook, Yap State, FSM, Unknown Craftsman*
Mother of pearl, tortoiseshell, bird feathers, coconut fiber twine, 2" long, twentieth century
Handmade hooks such as this one are still being made on Yap today.

FIGURE 83: *Machi Ritual Textile, Fais or Ulithi, Yap State, FSM, Unknown Weaver*
Banana fiber, natural dyes, 60" x 20," 1950s–1960s
The *machi* is a complex, specialized textile still made on Fais Island. Those made today look almost identical to the hundred-year-old examples found in some American museums. Made from a combination of un-dyed banana fiber with a weft of hibiscus fiber yarns dyed with mineral or vegetable pigments, the *machi* formerly had many important cultural roles. It was once used at the investiture of chiefs, as a burial shrouds for important persons, and as dance costumes at coming-of-age initiations for boys. *Machi* were generally viewed as the most valuable handmade object produced on the island and were traditionally considered to belong to the paramount chief (Feldman and Rubinstein 1986:60–61).

FIGURE 84: *Photograph*
Giant wheels of Yapese stone money are among the most famous forms of money in the world. This photo depicts a "bank" of Yapese money—a series of giant *rai* have been leaned against an ancient stone wall. Despite the fact that these giant stones have remained in this position for many years, their current owners are well known and recognized by the community. The photograph was taken by Edward Lashua in Yap, in association with the installation of a signaling station in 1964.

FIGURE 85: *Stone Money, Yap State, FSM, Unknown Maker*
Crystallized Calcite, 7½" x 6¾" and 6½" x 5½," 1965, 1950s
These two pieces of Yapese money represent the smallest denomination one *rai*. The first piece was given to Albert Miller, Jr. in 1965 in appreciation for the gift of a bicycle. The second piece was obtained from the Hogan estate. Crystals can be clearly seen on the second piece of money, while the first piece shows signs of chipping and wear. Whether these pieces had been actually used as currency would take an expert evaluation. Real money can no longer be taken from Yap State without obtaining special permission.

FIGURE 86: *Yar or Shell Money, Yap State, FSM, Unknown Maker*
Gold-lipped clamshell, coconut fiber twine, 10" x 4," 2003
This type of shell money, called a *yar* is worth less than those whose sides are broken off after being heated in hot sand. This example was probably made explicitly for trade since genuine, older examples can no longer be removed from the island.

FIGURE 87: *Two Skeins of Rope, Yap State, FSM, Unknown Makers*
Two skeins of coconut fiber rope, 50' and 100' long, 1972 and 2006
Although these two skeins of rope were made over thirty years apart, they look almost identical. Carefully twisted skeins like this were a valuable medium of exchange in historic times, when passing ships needed to replace their rigging. The Yapese are famous for the quality of their rope, which they make by twisting it together and rolling it over the thighs. This is often an activity of older men while they hang about the canoe house.

FIGURE 88: *Mother and Child, Republic of Palau, Heinrich*
Wood, mother of pearl, 18" high x 8" wide, 1960s
This statue was collected during the 1960s when the seller's parents were some of the first teachers to come to Palau under the American Administration. The figure, which may represent a mother taking part in the First Child Ceremony, wears a carved necklace representing a piece of Palauan bead money.

FIGURE 89: *Toluk or tortoiseshell money, Republic of Palau, Unknown Maker*
Tortoise shell, 5" x 3½" and 8" x 5," 1960s
These dishes, made by specialists using carved wooden molds, are still a form of "money" exchanged, usually by women at events such as marriages and funerals.

FIGURE 90: *Chuukese "Bull Horn" Clubs, Chuuk State, FSM, Unknown Carver*
Wood, 28" x 3¼," 1950s
These finely carved clubs with "bull horn" spikes carved along the middle are evocative of the fierce reputation of Chuukese warriors in early times. These clubs came from the Hogan estate.

FIGURE 91: *Shell Adzes, Yap State, FSM, Unknown Craftsman*
Tridacna shell, coconut sennit twine, wood, 15" and 21," 2002, 1960s
Shell was the only material for adze blades available on many Micronesian islands, and was used for making canoes and other carvings. Today, on Yap, adzes continue to be made, although the bindings on the older of the two examples shown here is more tightly structured. The adze obtained in 2002 may have been hafted solely for the tourist trade, another example of simplification.

FIGURE 92: *"Love Sticks", Chuuk State, FSM, Unknown Carvers*
Wood, black pigments, 12½" to 36½" long, 1950s to 1970s
The assortment of "love sticks" shown here illustrates the dramatic changes in both form and decoration which this object has gone through. These items are sometimes called "courting sticks" or "courting wands" and are called *fánáy* in the native language. The incised stick was described during the German and Japanese periods. The central stick, without incised design but with a similar shape and almost identical length to the incised example, may represent a transitional form. The largest "love stick," the form generally seen today, appears sturdy enough to have evolved from a club or another type of hand weapon.

FIGURE 93: *Dance Paddles, Pohnpei, FSM, Unknown Carvers*
Wood, natural fibers, black pigments, 17½"to 41" long, 1950s–1980s
These dance paddles were carved from soft, light-colored woods and incised with intricate designs reminiscent of those on "courting sticks," or *fánáy* (Goodenough 2002:252), and *tapuanu* masks in Chuuk. A trend of simplification can be seen on

these paddles. They have not been arranged by age, but older paddles can generally be identified as being larger, having a greater number of fiber tufts along the sides (although German period paddles also vary in number of tufts) and having more elaborate incised decorations. These items are another good example of simplification.

FIGURE 94: *"Courting Stick/Wand" or "Love Stick", Chuuk State, FSM, Unknown Carver*
Wood, pigment, 24½," 1950s
This early style of "love stick" is incised with an elaborate design.

FIGURE 95: *Photograph*
Taken in 1972, in Puluwat, Chuuk State, FSM, this photograph shows the carver Piong crafting a war club. His enlarged earlobes and the dolphin tattoos on his legs hark back to earlier times. This photograph is from the Belau National Museum collection and was made available courtesy of the Micronesian Seminar.

FIGURE 96: *Marshall Island Flowers, Republic of the Marshall Islands, Takien*
Kimej fibers, wire, wrappings, 1980s
A woman named Takien, who lived at Ron Ron on Majuro Atoll, is credited with having invented *kimej* flowers after WWII (Curtis 1986:47). Such flowers have become a whole new area for creative expression and are used to decorate purses, head *lei*, hats, and baskets. Brightly dyed, they often incorporate teneriffe patterns or use looping.

FIGURE 97: *Fans and Head Lei*
Shown here is an assortment of Marshall Islands fans and head *lei* in bright, intricate designs. The head *lei* and fans, especially those including inserts of tortoiseshell, date from the 1940s through the late 1960s.

FIGURE 98: *Postcard*
This hand-colored, Japanese period postcard, probably originally from the early 1930s, shows a group of young Caroline Islanders from Saipan wearing wraparound skirts made from trade cloth. Their necklaces, head *lei*, and belts represent more traditional adornments.

FIGURE 99: *Photograph*
Dressed in elaborate dance costumes for the Ninth Festival of Pacific Arts, a lead dancer and a dance director from Ebeye in the Marshall Islands pose between performances. This photograph was taken in 2004 by the author.

FIGURE 100: *Marshall Islands Mat, Republic of the Marshall Islands, Unknown Weaver*
Natural and dyed fibers, 42½" square, 1970s
This Marshall Islands mat has embroidered overlays in orange, green, and purple dyed natural fibers on the innermost portion of the mat's border. Many of these designs are again being woven due to a renewed interest in plaiting traditional mats.

FIGURE 101: *Lave Lava, Ulithi or Fais, Yap State, FSM, Unknown Weaver*
Banana fiber, dye, 62" (including fringe) x 21¼," 1950s–1960s
This skirt with rows of black and cream stripes is a fairly traditional design used for everyday wear. The border of the stripes, colored red in this example, varies so that individual weavers can be identified.

FIGURE 102: *Photograph*

This photograph, taken by Carlos Viti in the 1970s in Puluwat, Chuuk, shows men pushing an outrigger canoe out to sea wearing cotton loincloths. This photograph was made available courtesy of the Micronesian Seminar.

FIGURE 103: *Lava lava, Ulithi, Yap State, FSM, Unknown Weaver*
Banana and hibiscus fibers, dyes, 1960s

Most *lava lava* woven for day-to-day wear consist of strips that run the length of the cloth. However, this extremely detailed example has bands of geometric patterns woven crossways, which extend the length of the cloth and are reminiscent of those used on the *machi*.

FIGURE 104: *Machi, Ulithi or Fais, Yap State, FSM, Unknown Weaver*
Banana and hibiscus fibers, dyes, 1950s

This close up of a *machi* shows the intricately woven designs, which define this important textile. (Also see Figure 83.)

FIGURE 105: *Marshall Islands Necklace, Republic of the Marshall Islands, Unknown Jewelry Designer*
Woven fiber, white alu shells, cats eye, 1980s–1990s

This style of pendant has been popular for a number of years and recently has also been made and sold as a brooch.

FIGURE 106: *Photograph*

An artist proudly displays her beadwork in the CMNI booth at the Ninth Festival of Pacific Arts in Palau 2004. This photograph was taken by the author.

FIGURE 107: *Saipan Beaded Necklace, Saipan, CNMI, Bead Artist (See Figure 106.), Glass beads, 2004*

This necklace was purchased at the Ninth Festival of Pacific Arts in Palau in 2004 and was made by an artist from Saipan. There is a Carolinian tradition of making large collars in bold color designs using glass seed beads. This has become part of the identifying costume of Caroline Islanders in Saipan, as well as some islands between Yap and Chuuk. Men seem to wear larger more imposing collars, which can reach from shoulder to shoulder.

FIGURE 108: *Marshall Islands Necklace, Republic of the Marshall Islands, Unknown Jewelry Designer*
Woven fiber, snake head cowries, brown alu shells, 2004

Marshall Island women are justly famous for their talent in jewelry design. They incorporate many different types of cowries and natural fiber into necklaces and sometime into bracelets and earrings.

FIGURE 109: *Assorted Head Lei and Hats, Republic of the Marshall Islands, Jitiam Silk and Other Weavers*
Pandanus, kimej, dyes, assorted sizes, 1960s–2004

Marshall Islands head *lei* called *wut* are made in a variety of styles. In the 1960s, head *lei* were narrow with a crown of *alu* shells and an elaborate design woven into the head band. More recently, head *lei* have had beautifully woven and knotted flowers incorporated, like this example by Jitiam Silk, which was purchased at the Ninth Festival of Pacific Arts in Palau in 2004 and can be seen on the wicker head to the right.

FIGURE 110: *Belt, Outer Islands, Yap State, FSM, Unknown Maker*
Shell beads, tortoiseshell spacers, coconut sennit twine, 56" including ends, 1950s
These belts are very rare in the islands today and are treasured as valuable family heirlooms. Souvenir belts are currently being produced in the same pattern using black and white glass beads. This belt comes from the Hogan estate.

FIGURE 111: *Photograph*
Taken in Ulithi, probably in the 1950, this photo shows two girls preparing for a dance. They are painting their faces with red spots of turmeric and are wearing thin dance skirts over their striped wrap around *lava lava*. The traditional belts, made from tortoiseshell and handmade shell beads, are considered family heirlooms and scarce today.

FIGURE 112: *Pohnpei Sash or Tor, Pohnpei, FSM, Unknown Weaver*
Banana and hibiscus fibers, 66" long (including fringe), mid-1800s
This finely woven textile was made on a back strap loom in the same way *lava lava* are woven today and worn as a sash over a grass skirt. This *tor* is quite an early example, which was obtained from a collection in England.

FIGURE 113: *Hair Comb, Yap State, FSM, Unknown Maker*
Mangrove wood, 11½" long, 1950s
This style of comb, or *richib* meaning pin or nail, is made from pieces of mangrove wood pinned together. The size of this comb was once an indicator of the status of the wearer but these combs are no longer being made today.

FIGURE 114: *Hair Comb, Unknown Specialist*
Mangrove root, natural twine, 11½" long, 2004
This men's dance comb or *yep* was a gift from one of the Yapese chiefs at the conclusion of the Ninth Festival of Pacific Arts in Palau in 2004. This style of comb is quite fragile and does not last long. Currently, a specialist must be paid at least 30 dollars to make the comb.

FIGURE 115: *Marshall Islands Hair Clip, Republic of the Marshall Islands, Unknown Weaver*
Kimej fibers, metal clip, wrappings, 1980s
This hair clip came from a group of materials, which was originally displayed in a souvenir shop in Hawai'i and ended up in storage in Florida. The hair ornaments are all tightly woven using coconut fibers or *kimej* which has been attached to a metal clip. The group of hair clips included creative designs such as one with the colors of the Marshall Islands flag and the words "Air Marshall" embroidered on it.

FIGURE 116: *Basket, Kosrae State, FSM, Unknown Maker*
Natural fibers, commercial dyes, 8" circumference, 1950s
This mid-twentieth-century basket is interesting due to the absence of teneriffe. This basket could have also been made in the Marshall Islands and may be derivative of an earlier style of basket construction.

FIGURE 117: *Basketry Tray, Republic of the Marshall Islands, Unknown Maker*
Natural fibers, commercial dyes, gold-ringer cowries, tortoiseshell, 18," 1960s
This tray is an example of those made before the importation of tortoiseshell to the U.S. was banned. Today teneriffe patterns tend to be substituted for the tortoiseshell medallions which in this example have been inserted into the floor of the basket.

FIGURE 118: *Basketry Tray, Republic of the Marshall Islands, Unknown Weaver*
Kimej, maan, commercial dyes, money cowries, 17" long, late 1980s, early 1990s
This basket is an example of the creative scope of Marshallese weavers, evoking trees reflected in the water against a brilliant horizon. It was collected on Kwajalein Atoll by Nell Amador who was stationed there in the late 1980s early 1990s.

FIGURE 119: *Palauan Baskets or "Tet", Republic of Palau, Unknown Weavers*
Natural and dyed fibers
The *tet* is a basket used by Palauans to hold betel nut chew and other personal items. Commonly the *tet* is carried under the arm but baskets in a more conventional purse shape with handles and cowry shell closures are also produced. These baskets were provided through the generosity of William E. Perryclear, a photographer on Palau.

FIGURE 120: *Handbag, Republic of the Marshall Islands, Unknown Weaver*
Pandanus and other fibers, 9½" wide x 6" high excluding handle, 1980s
This Marshall Island handbag incorporates geometric patterns based on designs found in traditional mats. The interior is usually lined in tropical cloth or a plain woven liner.

FIGURE 121: *Handbag, Kili, Republic of the Marshall Islands, Unknown Weaver*
Kimej, reinforcing and lining material, 6" square excluding handles, 1970s
This handbag made by Bikini Islanders who moved to Kili Atoll during the 1960s is very finely woven and takes at least two weeks to make. These bags come in a variety of shapes and are sometimes decorated with teneriffe flowers.

FIGURE 122: *Betel Nut Bag, Yap State, FSM, Unknown Weaver*
Pandanus, 14" wide, late 1940s
Bags like this are called *waey* in Yap and are carried by everyone, mostly to hold betel nut paraphernalia. There are several similar types of these bags, some are made especially to be given as gifts, others are woven of young coconut leaves, among other materials. Such bags are an important accessory of Yapese daily life.

FIGURE 123: *Land Snail Purse, Guam, Unknown Maker*
Croqueted thread, satin lining, cardboard internal support, pink white and beige fat Guam partula, 1940s–1960s
These very attractive handbags make good use of the different colors of fat Guam partula to create their patterns. Sadly, the popularity of such bags led to the decline of the Guam land snail, and these purses are no longer being made.

FIGURE 124: *Pal Malem Fans, Malem District, Kosrae State, FSM, Jada Joseph and Mary Moses*
Pandanus fiber and commercial dyes, 12" to 14½," 1994
Made in the Malem District of Kosrae the intricate patterns around the face of these fans is said to replicate men's clothing.

FIGURE 125: *Kosrae Fan, Republic of Marshall Islands/Kosrae, FSM, Unknown Weaver*
Pandanus and coconut fiber, commercial dyes, 12½" long, 1940s–1950s
This is an early example characterized by an extremely tight, intricate, and elaborate handle and border design. (See Figures 12 and 13 for additional details.)

FIGURE 126: *Pal Tok Fans, Kosrae State, FSM, Brine Maeka*
Pandanus and coconut fiber, commercial dyes, both 15" long, 1992
This style of fan called *"pal tok"* or "sunburst" is said to have been introduced to Kosrae by Marshall Islanders during the Japanese Occupation around the time of WWII.

FIGURE 127: *Fire Fan, Republic of Palau, Unknown Maker*
Natural fiber, 12½" long, 2004
Fans similar to this one were made in nearly every island group and often in distinctive forms which have remained unchanged for over one-hundred years. These fans were made quickly in the bush to get a fire going.

FIGURE 128: *Hand Fan, Republic of the Marshall Islands, Unknown Makers*
Coconut, pandanus fibers, kimej, commercial dyes, 13½"and 15," 1980s–present day
This obovate style of fan is still being made in the Marshall Islands. The beautiful teneriffe flower designs placed at the center of fan face mirror those in contemporary Marshall Islands baskets and wall trays. The two fans with more elaborate handle designs date to the late 1980s, while the blue fan was woven more recently.

FIGURE 129: *Hand Fan, Pohnpei, FSM, Unknown Makers*
Coconut, hibiscus and pandanus fibers, tortoiseshell, feathers 15" to 17" long, 1945–1960s
These are all good examples of mid-twentieth century Pohnpei fans with round fan faces, round tortoiseshell inserts, feathers dyed in contrasting, alternating colors, and relatively simple handle designs.

FIGURE 130: *Hand Fan, Pohnpei, FSM, Unknown Makers*
Coconut, pandanus fibers, strips of plastic, commercial dyes and feathers, money cowries 14" (including feathers), 1980s–present
This style of fan, still made in Pohnpei, represents the modern alternative to the use of tortoiseshell inserts. Shells provide detail in the woven center. Sometimes fiber is used as a fringe, but more often feathers alternate white and sections of bright color. The handle can be plain or a simple checkered pattern. The fan's face can assume various shapes including round, obovate, and an upside down triangle consisting of three circular discs. This example reflects the process of material assimilation, since strips of white plastic have been incorporated into parts of the fan instead of natural fibers.

FIGURE 131: *Hand Fan, Guam, Unknown Maker*
Coconut fibers, dye, 12" long, late 1940s, early 1950s
This interesting diamond-shaped hand fan came from the estate of Irwin Kyle Vandam, a naval commander who later became a Trust Territory administrator and lived in Guam in the early 1950s. (Also see Figure 133 below.)

FIGURE 132: *Hand Fans, Republic of the Marshall Islands, Unknown Makers*
Feathers, tortoiseshell, commercial dyes, coconut and pandanus fibers, wood (handle), 15" to 17" long, 1945–1960s
This group of largely obovate fans contains beautiful examples of fans produced in the Marshall Islands after WWII and through the 1960s. Intricate teneriffe patterns are combined with tortoiseshell inserts in many configurations including heart shaped, round, or triangular. Feather fringes shown on two examples, are vulnerable to moths and are often damaged if not stored carefully. Two of the nine fans show the popular handle design of diamonds and squares.

FIGURE 133: *Hand Fan Kosrae State, FSM, Unknown Makers*
Coconut, pandanus fibers, commercial dyes, 12½"and 13½," 1980s, 1994
The diamond-shaped hand fan has a very broad distribution throughout Micronesia, though minor stylistic differences help identify the place of origin of individual fans. Examples from Kosrae have double points on their horizontal ends, while Pohnpei fans usually have single points. Kosrae fans usually include more elaborately woven designs than Pohnpei fans.

FIGURE 134: *Hand Fan, Republic of the Marshall Islands, Unknown Maker*
Coconut leaf, natural dyes, 16," 1890s, early 1900s
This fan was deaquisitioned from the Academy of Sciences Museum in San Francisco which was founded in 1853. A paper label on the fan says "Caroline Islands" but Linda Le Geyt nearly always identifies this fan as being from the Marshall Islands. This style of fan continues to be used in the traditional fan dance with modern variations.

FIGURE 135: *Storyboard: Demei and the Crocodile, Republic of Palau, Unknown Carver*
Wood, commercial paints, 36" x 7¼," 1950s
This board has active agitated figures and depicts a one dimensional side view of the *bai*. Both of these attributes are characteristics of an early board. Transitioning from the new style boards, this carver experimented with painting the back ground white and using additional colors. Demei and the Crocodile is a historic story about a man who went down to the water near the *bai* to use the bathroom and was bitten by a sea going crocodile. The board depicts the dramatic crocodile hunt which follows.

FIGURE 136: *Object Group*
Objects shown here were collected by Hera Ware Owen. Along with her husband, Robert Owens, the staff entomologist, Hera stayed in Palau from 1949 to 1978. The statue of a female figure (18½" high) is a rare example of carving by the Palauan carver Ngerbehid. The Palauan food bowl (14½" x 13½") was purchased at the annual craft fair, while the excellent early example of a Marshall Islands outrigger or korkor (14¾" x 13½" wide and 16" tall) was restored by the author's father-in-law Harry Lamberty.

FIGURE 137: *Incised Shell: The Aimelik Snake, Larry Kitalong*
Shell, handmade twine, 9¼" x 6" (not including twine), 2004
This incised shell tells the story of the Aimelik snake who, after terrorizing everyone, was finally defeated by a young man who put hot stones in the monster's mouth. Large shells like this one are now being used instead of tortoiseshell, which was pierced and inscribed with story board scenes through the 1960s.

BACK COVER: *Photograph*
This photograph, made available by Dr. Don Rubinstein, was taken in 1972 and shows a Fais man and a group of boys carrying a canoe to safety inland in preparation for a typhoon.

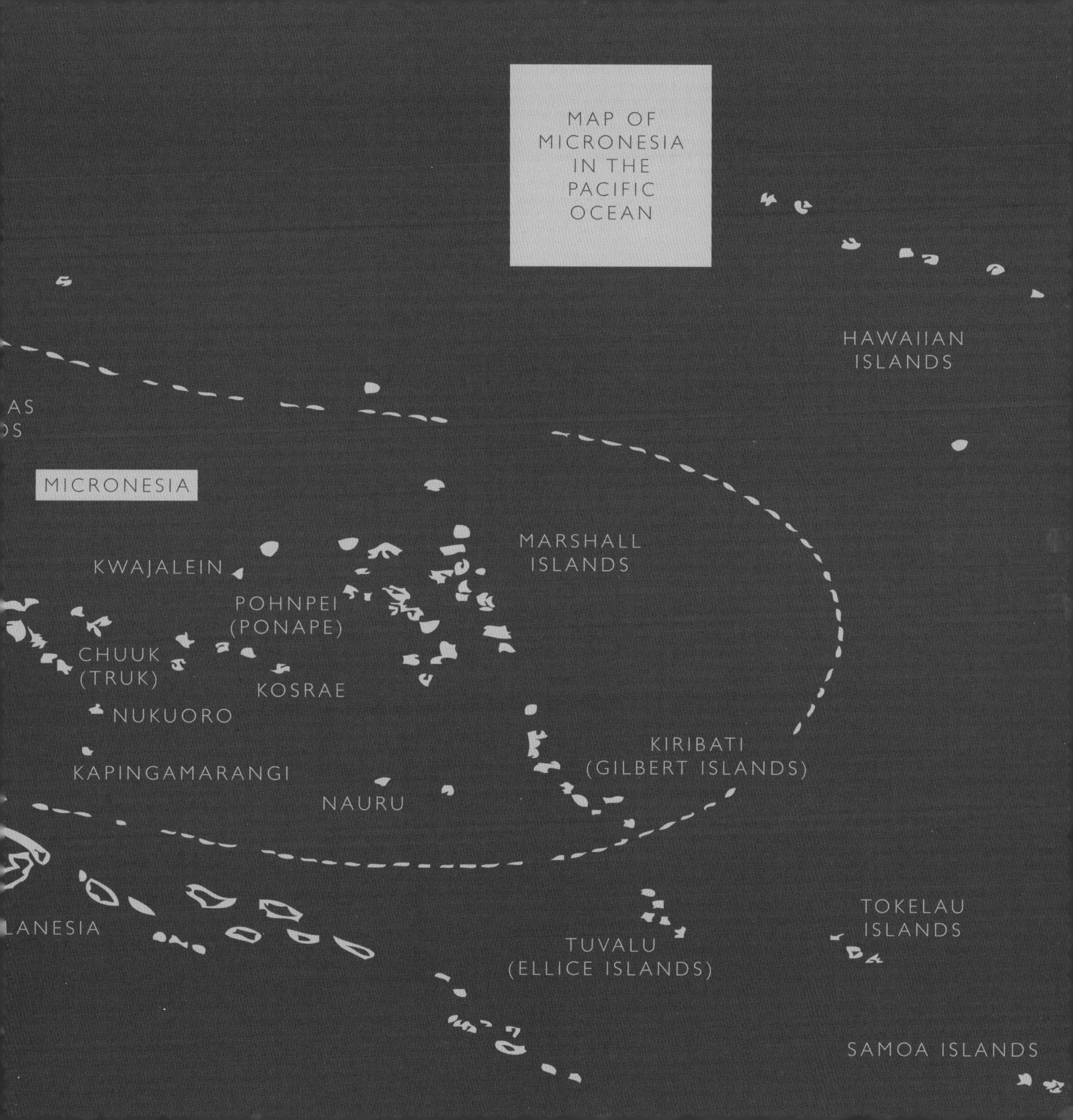

MAP OF
MICRONESIA
IN THE
PACIFIC
OCEAN

HAWAIIAN
ISLANDS

AS
OS

MICRONESIA

MARSHALL
ISLANDS

KWAJALEIN

POHNPEI
(PONAPE)

CHUUK
(TRUK)

KOSRAE

NUKUORO

KIRIBATI
(GILBERT ISLANDS)

KAPINGAMARANGI

NAURU

LANESIA

TOKELAU
ISLANDS

TUVALU
(ELLICE ISLANDS)

SAMOA ISLANDS